Human Psychology and Economic Fluctuation

Human Psychology and Economic Fluctuation

A New Basic Theory of Human Economics

Hideaki Tamura

330.019
T15h

First published 2006 by
PALGRAVE MACMILLAN
Houndmills, Basingstoke, Hampshire RG21 6XS and
175 Fifth Avenue, New York, N. Y. 10010
Companies and representatives throughout the world

PALGRAVE MACMILLAN is the global academic imprint of the Palgrave
Macmillan division of St. Martin's Press, LLC and of Palgrave Macmillan Ltd.
Macmillan® is a registered trademark in the United States, United Kingdom
and other countries. Palgrave is a registered trademark in the European
Union and other countries.

ISBN–13: 978–0–230–00482–5 hardback
ISBN–10: 0–230–00482–2   hardback

This book is printed on paper suitable for recycling and made from fully
managed and sustained forest sources.

A catalogue record for this book is available from the British Library.

Library of Congress Cataloging-in-Publication Data

Tamura, Hideaki, 1962-
    Human psychology and economic fluctuation : a new basic theory of
human economics / Hideaki Tamura.
        p. cm.
    Includes bibliographical references and index.
    ISBN 0–230–00482–2 (cloth)
    1. Marginal utility. 2. Demand (Economic theory) 3. Business
cycles–Psychological aspects. I Title.

HB201.T332 2006
330.01'9–dc22   2006041637

10   9   8   7   6   5   4   3   2   1
15   14 13 12 11 10 09 08 07 06

Printed and bound in Great Britain by
Antony Rowe Ltd, Chippenham and Eastbourne

To my parents and my grandmother

Contents

Chapter 6 The Effectiveness of Aggregate Demand Management Policy

Chapter 7 Dynamic Analysis of Demand Psychology and Policy Implications

List of Tables

List of Figures

Preface

The inspiration for this book—which advocates a more humanistic approach to economics that clarifies the direct relationship between human desire (diminishing utility) and economic fluctuations—derives from my efforts to explore universal and fundamental principles of human behavior in the context of a Robinson Crusoe desert island economy (considering both non-monetary and monetary frameworks). In the process of this research, I came to realize that the inevitable decline in the level of utility (satisfaction) that occurs with the passage of time is a fundamental driver of demand with important ramifications for a number of economic variables, and that the construction of economic models capable of tracking the changes in human desire that lie behind various observable phenomena is essential in order to improve the analytical capability of economic theory.

The concept of diminishing utility that provides the theoretical foundation for this book might appear somewhat empirical and subjective by comparison with the ordinal utility approach of modern economic analysis, but I believe that it enables analysis to be performed in a manner that better reflects human nature, and thus has the potential to improve the standing of economics as a truly "social" science by shedding valuable light on the nature of the business cycle and thereby enabling more accurate forecasts and more appropriate policy choices.

The pioneering work of J. B. Say (1836) did make some reference—albeit indirect—to the concept of diminishing utility, but the framework presented in this book is otherwise based entirely on my own ideas and deliberations. Further, the study reflects my own practical experience and observations as a bank employee in the disheartening post-bubble economic period known as "the lost decade" in Japan, and should be particularly evident from my discussions of the revised "credit multiplier" theory (Chapter 4), the process by which financial bubbles are created and destroyed (Chapter 5), and the effectiveness of discriminatory spending policy (Chapter 7).

My views may appear somewhat dogmatic at times, and my analytical assumptions and expositions may be flawed, inadequate, or perhaps downright mistaken in places due to a lack of technical expertise. I will therefore be most grateful for any criticism or comments from my readers, and will endeavor to ensure that all such feedback is reflected in future editions of this book as well as future branches of my research.

It has been the author's intention in this book to express his personal opinions and he alone takes full responsibility for its contents. In case of necessity, the author can be reached at: h.tamura@jupiter.ocn.ne.jp

I would like to take this opportunity to express my gratitude to all those who have made this book possible.

I must begin by thanking my father, who majored in economics at Japan's Ritsumeikan University and taught me—when I was still just a child—to look at things from an "economic" perspective by explaining concepts such as a product's "added value". More importantly still, my father taught me the existence of two different philosophies, "materialism" and "idealism". These views—especially "idealism"—aroused my imagination, leading me to explore ways of incorporating human desire into economic analysis. Such ideas have played a major role in enabling me to develop a "basic human accounting" framework that combines cycles for goods, labor, and money with a consideration of human desire.

I must also note the importance of Henderson and Quandt's *Microeconomic Theory: A Mathematical Approach* (second edition published by McGraw-Hill, 1971), from which I learnt the fundamentals of microeconomic analysis back in my student days. In particular, I would not have been able to formalize my theory of diminishing utility (based on my "basic human accounting" framework) without the knowledge that I gained from this book regarding optimization techniques in neoclassical economic theory and their practical applications.

My sincere gratitude also goes to Emeritus Professor Tsutomu Okawa of Osaka City University, who kindly read through my manuscript, provided useful advice and, furthermore, checked the numerical formulae using "Mathematica".

In addition, I would like to thank Language Resources Ltd., Kobe, Japan—in particular, Mr. Geoff Rupp and Mr. Murdoch MacPhee—for their assistance in the preparation of the English-language version of this book.

Finally, I must thank Palgrave Macmillan—in particular, Mrs. Amanda Hamilton and Miss Katie Button—for recognizing the value of this book and for seeing it through to publication.

This book is dedicated to the memory of my late grandmother and to my father, mother, and other members of my family who have provided me with such great support at all stages.

Hideaki Tamura

November 2005

Introduction

This book aims to construct a theoretical framework for the study of economics that better reflects the importance of various psychological factors and the causal connections between them. In other words, our goal is to improve the ability of economic theory to analyze various economic phenomena by explicitly modeling those elements of human desire that represent the true essence of any economy. For the purposes of this book, the phrase "human psychology" refers to the fundamental desire of human beings for consumption goods.

Modern economic theory does not make allowance for these sorts of psychological factors and causal connections, reasoning that they cannot be measured or that comparisons across individuals are impossible. In conducting my research, however, I have come to realize that this approach has limited the applicability of economic theory to various economic phenomena in a manner that has perhaps impeded further theoretical developments.

Existing economic theory provided no hint as to the disastrous future consequences of Japan's financial bubble of the late 1980s, and once the bubble had burst in the early 1990s, optimism was simply replaced by somewhat reactive attempts to explain what had happened. The failure of economic models to address psychological factors (and the causal connections between them) meant that the existing theory was unable to analyze or keep pace with the bubble economy's development and subsequent collapse, a macroeconomic phenomenon that I would argue was highly psychological in nature. This failure of economic theory is perhaps the primary reason that Japan's government was so slow to act.

Financial bubbles have wreaked havoc on capitalist economies on numerous occasions since Holland's "tulip bubble" of the 17th century, and it therefore seems obvious that the development of a theoretical framework capable of explaining the process by which bubbles are created and destroyed in a consistent fashion would be of great value to all those who live in capitalist economies.

In this book, I create a framework for analyzing economic cycles that incorporates the process by which people seek to fulfill their desires. Based on this framework, which I term the "human income-expenditure

1

balance", I demonstrate that there is a close and unbreakable relationship between various measurable economic phenomena and elements of human psychology, and argue that an analytical approach that neglects these psychological elements is likely to be of only limited utility from the perspective of economic forecasting.

I also argue that the extremely "psychological" process by which financial bubbles are formed and destroyed can be understood in terms of an analytical model that (properly) recognizes the interdependence of observable phenomena and elements of human psychology.

Analysis based on this "human income-expenditure balance" is far from difficult, and is consistent with traditional equilibrium analysis whereby consumers maximize utility and firms maximize profits. In Chapter 2 of this book, I introduce the concept of "diminishing utility" as a means of modeling human desire, and demonstrate that it is a relatively simple task to construct an analytical model that incorporates human psychology as a structural element.

It is my sincere hope that this book will convince economists of the need to take psychological factors into account when analyzing economic phenomena, and that this approach will be taken on board by economic forecasters and policymakers.

The book consists of eight chapters, a brief summary of which follows.

In Chapter 1, "The Human Income-Expenditure Balance", we look at the "human income-expenditure balance" in both a non-monetary economy (based on the "Robinson Crusoe model") and a monetary economy (a household/firm model), and argue that diminution of utility represents a fundamental driver of demand.

In Chapter 2, "Fundamentals of the Theory of Diminishing Utility", we introduce the concept of diminishing utility as a means of modeling human desire and outline other basic concepts that are to be used in our subsequent analysis.

In Chapter 3, "Analysis of a Non-Monetary Economy", we derive a "basic equation of labor" and outline a theory that enables the simultaneous determination of output (quantity) and resource allocation through a process of maximizing expected total utility (defined as the sum of expected utility from goods and utility of leisure) for an individual experiencing diminishing utility in a Robinson Crusoe (non-monetary) economy. We also consider how "commissioned labor" may arise as a result of a "rerouting" of the stock of capital goods and the impact of such labor on output of investment goods.

In Chapter 4, "Extension to Analysis of a Monetary Economy", we demonstrate that the "basic equation of labor" derived in Chapter 3 can also be used in analysis of a monetary economy based on a household/firm model, and complete our theoretical framework by introducing monetary elements.

In Chapter 5, "Human Psychology and Economic Fluctuation", we construct a theoretical model of endogenous business cycles and economic growth by removing certain previous assumptions relating to stability, thereby enabling us to demonstrate the direct relationship between human psychology (desire) and economic fluctuation. We also use the concept of diminishing utility to examine the mechanism by which financial bubbles are created and destroyed (a macroeconomic phenomenon).

In Chapter 6, "The Effectiveness of Aggregate Demand Management Policy", we use the concept of diminishing utility to construct a theoretical model for aggregate demand management policy (monetary and fiscal policy), and then use this model to examine the potential impact of policy action on the labor market, goods market, and money market (as well as the interaction between these markets).

In Chapter 7, "Dynamic Analysis of Demand Psychology and Policy Implications", we apply the concept of diminishing utility to a dynamic analysis of demand psychology in which each household considers the amount it is prepared to spend on "reconsumption" of goods. We also consider economic stimulus measures that are likely to be highly effective from a short-term perspective.

In Chapter 8, "A Summary of Our Theoretical Framework", I conclude this book by summarizing the characteristics of the theory of diminishing utility from the perspectives of macroeconomic and microeconomic theories, and present some materials that may help readers to gain a better understanding of my framework. I also discuss some important issues—such as underemployment equilibrium analysis—that I have been unable to consider in sufficient detail in this book.

The analysis in this book is based on a "closed economy" that conducts no foreign trade (exports/imports) and has no capital transactions with other nations. It should also be noted that for the sake of convenience, we use the term "goods" to include various services and other intangibles that can be consumed or used in production (for example, subcontracted manufacturing) in addition to physical goods and materials.

Other assumptions used in our analysis are explained in the relevant chapter or section.

Chapter 1

The Human Income-Expenditure Balance

In this chapter, we put together a "basic human accounting" framework that illustrates the interdependence of various "accounts"—utility, goods, (work) time, and money—with a view to illustrating the importance of various psychological factors and the causal connections between them. We then show that human "demand" derives not from exogenous income as determined by corporate and government investment and the initial allocation of production elements, but from the fact that the utility gained from goods inevitably declines over time. In other words, the concept of "diminishing utility" is at the heart of our analysis.

We begin by constructing an accounting framework for a subsistence economy in which money does not exist and the producer (firm) and the consumer (household) are the same entity (a non-monetary economy), and then move on to an exchange economy (monetary economy) in which money exists and goods, labor, and money are traded between a producer (firm) and consumer (household) which are separate entities. We assume that human satisfaction derives from two different types of utility: (1) utility obtained from the consumption of consumption goods ("utility from goods"); and (2) utility obtained from time spent resting ("utility of leisure").

This chapter is structured as follows. In Section 1, we derive the human income-expenditure balance for a non-monetary subsistence economy that is (loosely) based on the adventures of Robinson Crusoe.[1] In Section 2, we consider separate income-expenditure balances for a consumer (household) and a producer (firm), and then combine these—by allowing the exchange of goods, labor, and money—into the human income-expenditure balance for a monetary economy (a household/firm model). Section 3 concludes this chapter by arguing that the fundamental driver of demand (in either a non-monetary or monetary economy) is *diminishing utility*, and that analysis of human desire is therefore essential if we are to gain a better understanding of various economic phenomena.

1. The Human Income-Expenditure Balance in a Non-Monetary (Robinson Crusoe) Economy

1.1. Framework of Analysis

In this section we explore the basic relationship between human needs and the supply-demand balance (of consumption goods) by considering the case of a subsistence (island) economy populated by a single castaway known as Robinson Crusoe. Our analysis is based on the following assumptions:

(1) The only type of consumption goods available to Crusoe is fish.
(2) Crusoe obtains a quantity of fish that is proportional to the time for which he works.
(3) Any fish (consumption goods) caught during a given period of time are consumed during that same period of time (that is, consumption cannot be deferred).
(4) Crusoe's total utility is the sum of the utility gained from consuming fish and the utility gained from leisure (time spent not working).
(5) The island is populated by wild animals that will attack both Robinson and the fish on which he feeds.
(6) Immediately after being washed ashore, Crusoe does not have any fishing equipment such as a net or harpoon, nor does he have any materials with which to make weapons or shelter against external threats.

Given these assumptions, Crusoe must initially attempt to catch fish with his own hands (that is, he has a low productivity of labor), and when attacked by wild animals he must suspend his work (catching fish) or leisure and flee to a safe place.

I have chosen to begin with such an example so as to illustrate the dramatic improvement in labor productivity that was brought about by the development and use of tools, which may be viewed as a defining characteristic of mankind.

1.2. Diminishing Utility and Demand for Consumption Goods

In order to survive, all living beings must maintain a minimum average level of energy over a given period of time. Such energy is typically obtained through the consumption of food. In our example, Crusoe maintains the necessary level of energy by consuming fish (the only available consumption good).

It must be noted, however, that the level of energy obtained from a single meal cannot be maintained indefinitely. In other words, the level of energy derived from a single act of consumption declines with the passage of time (except in certain special cases). This is because the various activities of living beings require them to consume energy at a certain rate. If this energy is viewed as the utility associated with a given consumption good, then we may refer to the phenomenon whereby the level of utility declines with the passage of time as "diminution of utility". For the purposes of our subsequent discussion, we denote the (constant) rate at which utility declines over time by the symbol β.[2]

The amount by which Crusoe's utility declines over a period of time of length T may therefore be expressed as βT. This corresponds to the consumption of energy, and cannot be avoided so long as Crusoe remains alive. If we denote the number of fish caught by Crusoe during T units of time by q^c and the initial level of utility (energy) derived from each fish by α, then the amount of utility (energy) acquired during T units of time may be expressed as αq^c. It is this ability to acquire new energy that enables Crusoe to maintain—*on average*—a level of energy (utility) sufficient for survival, which may be denoted E_1 and referred to as "expected utility". The relationship between these variables is illustrated in Figure 1.1.

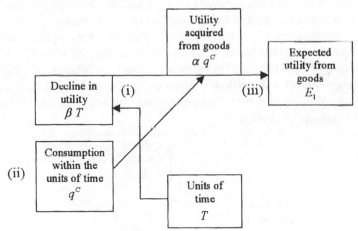

Figure 1.1 Causal relationship between variables related to diminishing utility

The diagram should be interpreted as follows:
(i) Crusoe receives T units of time, which may be allocated to work or leisure, but which require the expenditure of βT units of utility (energy).
(ii) Crusoe must acquire new energy to prevent a decline in the level of expected utility, and does so by consuming q^c units of fish.

(iii) Consumption of these fish enables Crusoe to maintain the necessary level of expected utility (E_1).

1.3. Allocation of Time and the Supply of Consumption Goods

We now consider the questions of how Crusoe allocates his time and how he goes about acquiring consumption goods (fish). Crusoe does not possess any weapons or shelter against external threats, and must allocate his sole resource—time—across three activities: (a) work; (b) protection of self against external threats; and (c) leisure.

(a) At this stage of our analysis, we assume that Crusoe spends all of his working time producing the consumption good (i.e. catching fish). Later we shall extend our analysis to include the possibility of producing investment goods (in this case, fishing equipment). Assuming that Crusoe has T units of time, we denote time spent working by T_L, and the quantity of fish caught (or supplied) in this time by the production function $q^c(T_L)$.

(b) Assumption (5) in Section 1.1 states that Crusoe may be attacked by wild animals. Crusoe lacks weapons and shelter, and must therefore suspend his work (catching fish) or leisure (resting) if attacked, and flee to a safe place. As such, time spent protecting himself against external threats is considered separately from "work" and "leisure".

(c) Leisure time is calculated by subtracting time spent working and time spent protecting himself against external threats from Crusoe's total allocation of time (T), and includes rest, sleep, fulfillment of other desires, and other activities that allow Crusoe to restore and maintain his capacity to work. We assume that Crusoe derives "utility of leisure" from time spent (invested) in this way.[3]

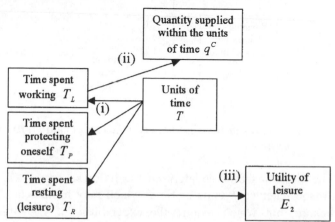

Figure 1.2 Causal relationship between variables related to allocation of time

In Figure 1.2, we denote "utility of leisure" by E_2 and illustrate how Crusoe apportions his T units of time as well as the causal connections between variables: (i) with the passage of time, Crusoe receives T units of time, which he then spends either working (T_L), protecting himself against external threats (T_P), or resting (T_R); (ii) Crusoe receives (supplies to himself) $q^c(T_L)$ units of the consumption good (fish) in exchange for the time that he spends working; (iii) Crusoe invests the time he has remaining after working and protecting himself in leisure, from which he derives utility $E_2(T_R)$.

1.4. The Human Income-Expenditure Balance (Basic Human Accounting)

Figure 1.3 is a flowchart that combines Figure 1.1 (which shows causal connections relating to utility from goods) and Figure 1.2 (causal connections relating to utility of leisure) by equating demand for the consumption good with the supply of the consumption good over the T units of time acquired by Crusoe.

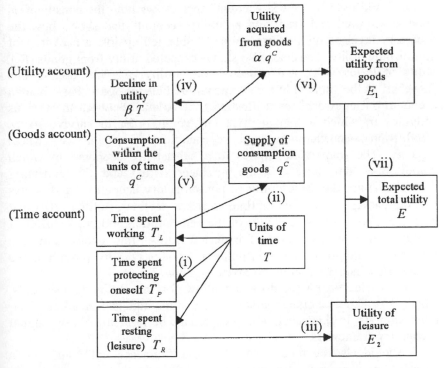

Figure 1.3 A primitive "human income-expenditure balance"

The diagram should be interpreted as follows:
(i) with the passage of time, Crusoe receives T units of time, which he then spends either working (T_L), protecting himself against external threats (T_P), or resting (T_R); (ii) Crusoe receives (supplies to himself) $q^c(T_L)$ units of the consumption good (fish) in exchange for the time that he spends working; (iii) Crusoe invests the time he has remaining after working and protecting himself in leisure, from which he derives utility $E_2(T_R)$; (iv) with the passage of time, Crusoe's utility diminishes by an amount equal to βT; (v) Crusoe must obtain utility from goods in order to offset this decline in utility, which in this case means that Crusoe must consume the consumption good (fish) that he has supplied to himself; (vi) by consuming the consumption good, Crusoe receives expected utility (E_1), which is the level of utility that he requires over the period in question; (vii) on average, over the period in question, Crusoe derives a total level of satisfaction (expected total utility E) equal to the utility of leisure (E_2) taken in accordance with (iii) plus the expected utility from goods (E_1) that derives from consumption in accordance with (vi).[4]

This flowchart consists of a "time account" that shows how time is acquired and used, a "goods account" that shows how the consumption good is acquired and used, and a "utility account" that shows how the necessary level of utility from goods is obtained against a backdrop of diminishing utility. The chart also shows expected utility from goods (E_1), utility of leisure (E_2), and expected total utility (E). We refer to this flowchart as the "human income-expenditure balance" or a "basic human accounting framework", as it illustrates the balance between the various activities in which a human must engage in order to survive: work (production), consumption, and regeneration of productive (work) capacity. The framework applies to a subsistence economy in which money does not exist and the producer (firm) and the consumer (household) are the same entity (a non-monetary economy), and shows that the passage of T units of time causes a decline in utility (βT) that generates *demand* for a quantity of the consumption good (q^c) sufficient to maintain a positive level of expected utility from goods, and also generates a *supply* of the consumption good $q^c(T_L)$ by providing the producer/consumer with time to invest in labor (T_L).

This basic framework does not allow for the ability to use tools, which is perhaps the main characteristic that distinguishes mankind from other animals. In this sense, it could perhaps be termed a "basic animal accounting framework".

It should also be noted that while the "time account" and "goods account" are in balance, the "utility account" is not (that is, the decline in utility with the passage of time is not equal to the utility derived from goods). This is because the utility derived from goods (αq^c) must exceed the amount by which utility declines (βT)—that is, there must be a positive utility surplus—in order for the expected utility from goods to be positive $(E_1 > 0)$. As such, the "utility account" should be considered a "conceptual" account that encompasses the idea of *expected* utility from goods.

The fundamental driver of demand within our framework—the engine behind the economic cycle—is the decline in utility with the passage of time (βT). In other words, the key parameters are: (1) β, the (positive) rate at which utility declines $(\beta > 0)$; and (2) T, the amount of time that has passed $(T > 0)$. Obviously, the demand entity within our framework (Crusoe) can do nothing about the passage of time, so we are left with β, the (positive) rate at which utility declines, as the fundamental driver of demand. Note that in the case of an "uninteresting" consumption good for which β is equal to zero, there will be no decline in utility no matter how much time passes $(\beta T = 0)$, such that no new demand for the consumption good (in order to *maintain* a certain level of expected utility from goods) will be generated.

1.5. The Emergence of Tools, Deferred Consumption, and Basic Human Accounting

We now extend our framework to allow for: (a) the possibility of using tools; and (b) the possibility of deferring consumption to a later date. To this end, we remove Assumption (6) from Section 1.1, and assume that Crusoe—who has been struggling to catch fish with his bare hands—one day takes advantage of low tide to reach a shipwrecked vessel a short distance offshore, from which he recovers a harpoon and a fishing net, as well as guns and explosives that he uses to eliminate predators from the island, and material from the vessel that he uses to build a sturdy shelter. This means that Crusoe no longer needs to spend time protecting himself from external threats (T_P), as a result of which he has more time to allocate to work (T_L) and leisure (T_R). Use of the harpoon and fishing net also increases his work productivity, enabling him to catch more fish in a given period of time. We also remove Assumption (3) from Section 1.1, and assume that Crusoe can defer some consumption to a later date and maintain a stock of consumption goods (fish) as a buffer against future uncertainty.

Previously, we assumed that Crusoe devoted his entire work time to the process of catching fish. Now, however, he must set aside some time to sharpen or replace his harpoon tip and repair holes in his fishing net. Crusoe's fishing equipment can be viewed as a "capital good" (K), and we can then define the "capital attrition rate" (δ) to be the proportion of this capital good that is "lost" as a result of usage or the passage of time, and consider the quantity of "replacement investment goods" (q^{IR}) that must be added to the capital stock in order to maintain it at a level sufficient to support production. Crusoe is able to dramatically boost his work productivity (the quantity of fish that he can catch within a given period of time) by using the capital good (fishing equipment), but must also devote some of his work time to producing replacement investment goods in order to maintain the capital stock. However, as illustrated in Figure 1.4, the productivity gains resulting from the use of the capital good are more than enough to offset the time that must be spent producing replacement investment goods, such that Crusoe's average work productivity (measured as fish caught per unit of work time) increases as a result of access to the capital good (fishing equipment).

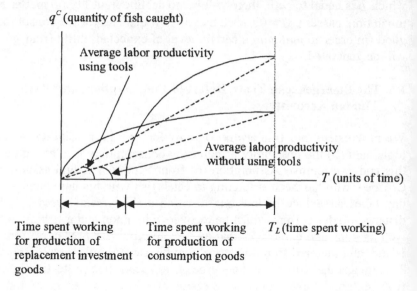

Figure 1.4 Impact of using tools on average labor productivity

We now consider the impact of removing Assumption (3) from Section 1.1 by dividing consumption into current-period consumption (consumption that takes place during the T units of time, denoted by $q^{c\,\prime}$) and deferred consumption (additions to the stock of consumption goods). It should be noted that only current-period consumption ($q^{c\,\prime}$) has an impact on current-period utility from goods.

Figure 1.5 is based on Figure 1.3, but reflects the existence of a capital stock, the need for a flow of replacement investment goods to cover capital attrition, the fact that Crusoe no longer needs to spend time

(T_P) to protect himself, and the existence of a stock of consumption goods that increases as a result of deferred consumption.

For the purpose of our flowchart, we capture the idea that some of Crusoe's work time is spent producing replacement investment goods by having him divide his total work output into consumption goods and replacement investment goods.

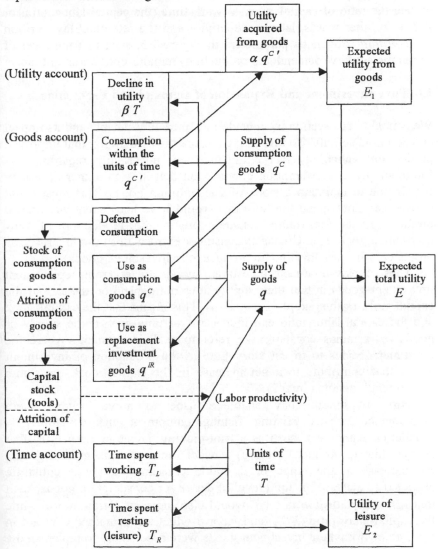

Figure 1.5 "Basic human accounting framework" that reflects capital stock (tools) and replacement investment

If we assume that utility declines at a constant rate (β) and that other circumstances remain unchanged, then the supply of goods (q) and the supply of work time (T_L) are also constants. Labor productivity also remains unchanged, because we assume that replacement investment goods are used only to maintain a sufficient capital stock to support production, and that no deliberate effort is made to either increase or reduce the ratio of capital stock to work time (the capital-labor ratio, or K/T_L). In other words, labor productivity and the rate of utility attrition are *constant* exogenous parameters in Figure 1.5, such that the level of economic activity (demand and production) remains constant over time.

1.6. Pure Investment and Expansion of Demand and Production

We conclude this section by considering "pure investment" and its impact on economic activity. To this end, we make the assumption that improved production technology has eliminated any uncertainty regarding the future supply of consumption goods, such that it is no longer necessary for Crusoe to maintain a stock of consumption goods. This means that Crusoe can now spend the time that would have been spent working to produce goods for future consumption in the production of new investment goods (i.e. Crusoe as consumer entrusts this time to Crusoe as producer, who uses this time to produce pure investment goods).

These newly-produced investment goods differ from replacement investment goods in that their supply does not depend on the size of the capital stock or the output of goods (q). This means that the capital stock and the capital-labor ratio can increase over time even if the supply of goods (q) remains constant. We refer to such investment—where the consumer decides to invest work time in the production of investment goods that contribute to a net increase in the capital stock—as "pure investment" (denoted by q^{IP}).

Pure investment may enable Crusoe to move beyond mere maintenance of his existing fishing equipment and develop new production equipment (such as a fruit-picking device or flour mill) that enables him to produce (acquire) a wider range of consumption goods. An increase in the range of desirable consumption goods could be expected to increase his total level of desire for consumption goods, such that his utility attrition rate (β) would also increase. Furthermore, while the capital-labor ratio (K/T_L) and labor productivity remained constant in our framework where investment goods were used solely to replenish the capital stock (Figure 1.5), pure investment would enable both the capital-labor ratio (K/T_L) and labor productivity to increase over time, thereby bringing about an increase in total output (supply).

In other words, the introduction of pure investment means that our exogenous parameters (labor productivity and the rate of utility attrition) both increase over time, such that economic activity (demand and production) increases with each new year as the supply side (labor productivity) keeps pace with the demand side (desire for consumption goods). A framework that incorporates pure investment is shown in Figure 1.6.

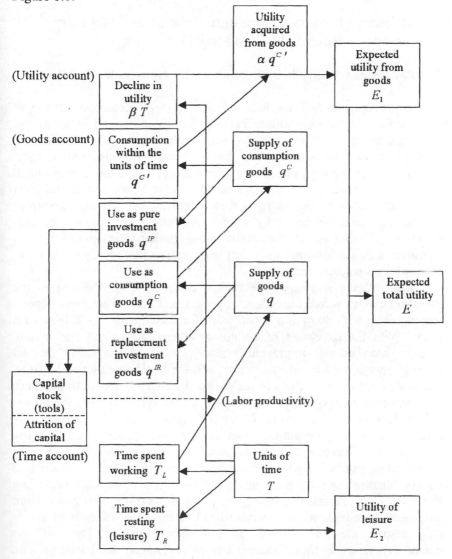

Figure 1.6 "Basic human accounting framework" that incorporates pure investment and its impact on economic activity

This concludes our examination of the "human income-expenditure balance" in a non-monetary economy.

Note that our framework is applicable not only to a single-person economy, but also to the "average" situation faced by members of subsistence economies (such as ancient societies or modern collectives) in which work is shared equally in the pursuit of a common goal (utility).

2. The Human Income-Expenditure Balance in a Monetary Economy (a Household/Firm Model)

2.1. The Role of Money in an Economy with Households and Firms

In the previous section we used the example of Robinson Crusoe to explore the income-expenditure balance for an individual or collective that owns the means of production (tools) and uses it to satisfy his/its own demand (desire) for consumption goods. Until the 16th century, most people were engaged in farming, stockbreeding, or fishing, and obtained the food and other goods they needed to support themselves and their dependents either by producing it themselves, or by exchanging surplus output for goods produced by others. As such, the "human income-expenditure balance" at that time could perhaps be modeled as a Robinson Crusoe economy or a simple extension that incorporates flows of surplus output between collectives.

However, the structure of a typical economy then changed as the capitalist classes seized the means of production away from most people, leaving them with no option but to work for the capitalist classes as paid labor. With the exception of certain geographical regions and certain people (such as self-employed farmers), most people today do not directly own any means of production, and are instead employed by firms established by the capitalist classes, using their wage income to purchase the consumption goods that they require. Firms typically own the means of production in the form of capital stock, earn (fair) profits by (efficiently) selling the output generated by paid workers, and then use these profits to increase their capital stock and expand sales.

In other words, people with no access to the means of production support themselves with wage income earned in exchange for providing firms with labor, using this income to purchase consumption goods from firms and thereby maintain a certain level of expected utility from goods (E_1) despite the phenomenon of diminishing utility. The same is essentially true of those individuals who happen to have become capitalists: such individuals provide firms with labor in the form of managerial services, in exchange for which they receive (for example) executive compensation and bonuses that they use to purchase consumption goods and thereby maintain a certain level of expected utility from goods (E_1) despite the phenomenon of diminishing utility. In summary, a monetary economy differs from our previous example of a non-monetary economy in that households (paid workers) and firms (owners of the means of production, or capital stock) are distinct entities, with activity in a monetary economy centering around flows of labor, consumption goods, and money between households and firms.

2.2. The Income-Expenditure Balance for Households and Firms Where Households Own the Stock of Consumption Goods

We can now begin the process of extending our "human accounting framework" to a monetary economy with a separate household and firm. As we did in the previous section, we initially assume that a household devotes all of its income to consumption (with any amounts that are not consumed during the T units of time being added to the stock of consumption goods) and does not undertake any pure investment.

We use the term "household" to refer to an individual paid worker, a capitalist, and their families, and define "household income" (W) as the total of wage income and capitalist income. We refer to the portion of household income that is devoted to current-period consumption as "household consumption" (C_W). In our non-monetary economy in Figure 1.5, the individual (or collective) was a consumer/producer that owned the means of production (tools), but in our household/firm framework, the corporate sector owns the means of production (tools) and produces investment goods and consumption goods using labor purchased from the household sector, while the household sector purchases consumption goods using household income received (from the corporate sector) in exchange for the provision of labor.

As such, the flows associated with the capital stock (including capital attrition) and the production function disappear from our previous (non-monetary) framework, and the household sector now receives household income W (in cash) in exchange for its provision of T_L units of labor (measured in terms of time), and devotes all of its income to consumption (including deferred consumption). These new additions are incorporated into a "money account" as shown in Figure 1.7, which is an adaptation of Figure 1.5 and shows the income-expenditure balance for the household sector in a monetary economy.

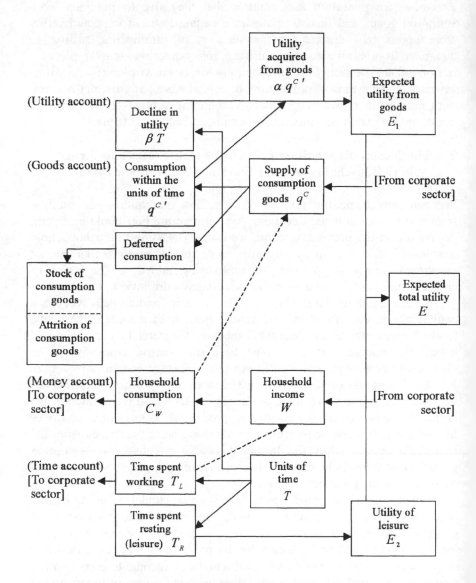

Figure 1.7 "Income-expenditure balance for the household sector" in a monetary economy

As was the case in our non-monetary economy, the household receives T units of time (with the passage of time), which it then spends either working (T_L) or resting (T_R), deriving utility of leisure (E_2) from the latter activity. However, as the household has neither a capital stock nor a production function (technology), the household receives its remuneration for work T_L as household income (W) rather than as goods. We assume that the household sector uses all of this income to purchase consumption goods from the corporate sector, consuming some of these goods within the T units of time and adding the remainder to its stock of consumption goods for future (deferred) consumption. Consumption within the T units of time provides the household with utility from goods sufficient to maintain a given level of expected utility from goods despite the phenomenon of diminishing utility.

In summary, the household sector receives satisfaction from its (average) consumption of consumption goods during the T units of time (measured as expected utility from goods E_1) as well as satisfaction from time spent resting and regaining its capacity to engage in productive work (measured as utility of leisure E_2), resulting in expected total utility (satisfaction) of E.

We next consider the income-expenditure balance for the corporate sector. In our monetary economy with distinct household and corporate entities, the corporate sector owns the means of production in the form of capital stock, earns (fair) profits by (efficiently) selling the output generated by paid workers, and then uses these profits to increase its capital stock and expand sales. As such, the flows associated with the capital stock (including capital attrition) and the production function that were shown in our non-monetary framework are now attributed to the corporate sector. The corporate sector produces goods by purchasing work time T_L (a production factor) from the household sector. The firm then sells these goods, and purchases (from itself) the amount necessary to replenish its capital stock, resulting in sales revenue I_R. The remaining production output is sold to the household sector as consumption goods, resulting in sales revenue C_W. Of this total sales revenue $(C_W + I_R)$ (from replacement investment goods and household consumption), the amount corresponding to I_R is considered corporate income (P) and used to fund depreciation costs, while the remaining amount is paid to the household sector as household income (W). This framework is shown in Figure 1.8.

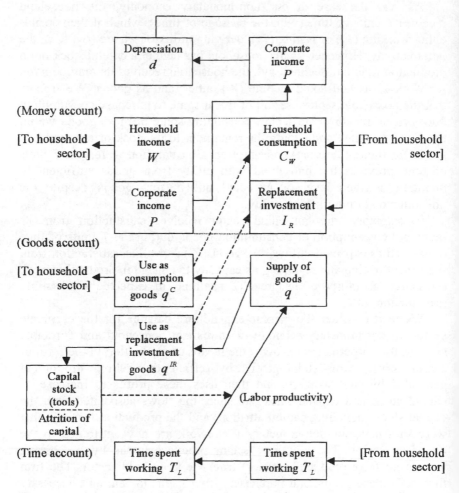

Figure 1.8 "Income-expenditure balance for the corporate sector" in a monetary economy

Figure 1.9 combines the income-expenditure balances for the household sector (Figure 1.7) and the corporate sector (Figure 1.8) for the case of zero pure investment. The household sector provides the corporate sector with work time T_L and sales revenue C_W (based on its purchases of consumption goods), while the corporate sector supplies the household sector with household income W and consumption goods q^c. Solid arrows depict transactions within the same "account" and direct input/output relationships (based on a linear production function etc.) between different accounts, while dotted arrows depict indirect relationships or interdependence between different accounts.

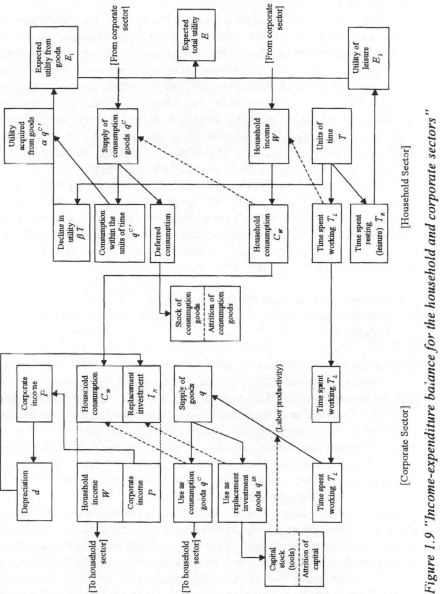

Figure 1.9 "Income-expenditure balance for the household and corporate sectors" in a monetary economy for the case of zero pure investment

Figure 1.9 may be viewed as the extension to a monetary economy (based on a household/firm model) of Figure 1.5, which showed the human income-expenditure balance for a non-monetary economy in which no pure investment takes place.

In Figure 1.9, all household income is used to purchase consumption goods (including goods set aside for future consumption), and the household sector does not decide to channel some of its income (q^{IP}) back to the corporate sector for use in pure investment. As such, the corporate sector does not undertake any pure investment, which means that on the demand side, there are no new consumption goods (or improved functionality) to cause an increase in the utility attrition rate. On the production side, replacement investment goods are used only to maintain a sufficient capital stock to support production, such that the capital-labor ratio (K/T_L) and labor productivity both remain unchanged.

In other words, labor productivity and the rate of utility attrition are *constant* exogenous parameters in Figure 1.9, such that the level of economic activity (demand and production) remains constant over time. The parameters facing the corporate sector also remain unchanged, such that the firm has no opportunity to earn net profits (that is, its income remains equal to its depreciation expenses).

2.3. The Income-Expenditure Balance for Households and Firms Where Some Consumption Goods Are Diverted for "Pure" Investment

We next consider a framework where the household sector entrusts part of its income (or consumption goods) to the corporate sector for use in pure investment. As we did in Section 1, we make the assumption that improved production technology has eliminated any uncertainty regarding the future supply of consumption goods, such that it is no longer necessary for the household to maintain a stock of consumption goods. This means that the portion of household income that was previously used to buy goods for future consumption can now be invested in the form of "household savings" (S_W).

The corporate sector issues shares and/or bonds, in exchange for which it receives all of the household sector's savings, which can then be used to fund new investment. This new investment yields the firm I_P in additional sales revenue, and enables the firm to channel some of its effort (purchased labor) into the production of new investment goods. These newly-produced ("pure") investment goods differ from replacement investment goods in that their supply does not depend on the size of the capital stock or the output of goods (q), which means that the capital stock and the capital-labor ratio can increase over time even if the supply of goods (q) remains constant. It should also be noted that the household (consumer) becomes a creditor through its purchases of shares and/or bonds, while the firm (producer) becomes a debtor.[5]

This pure investment activity enables the firm to provide new consumption goods or add new features or functionality to existing consumption goods. This serves to increase the household sector's total level of desire for consumption goods, such that its utility attrition rate (β) would also increase. Furthermore, by adding to the capital stock, pure investment would enable both the capital-labor ratio (K/T_L) and labor productivity to increase over time, thereby bringing about an increase in total output (supply).

In other words, the introduction of pure investment means that our exogenous parameters (labor productivity and the rate of utility attrition) both increase over time, such that economic activity (demand and production) increases with each new year and the firm is able to earn income in excess of its depreciation expenses. The firm's net income or corporate savings (S_P) is calculated by subtracting depreciation expenses and payments of share dividends and bond interest to the household sector from corporate income (P), and may be used in part to fund the firm's pure investment activity (I_P).

Figure 1.10 is an adaptation of Figure 1.9, and shows the income-expenditure balances for the household and corporate sectors in a monetary economy in which pure investment activity takes place. Figure 1.10 may be viewed as the extension to a monetary economy (based on a household/firm model) of Figure 1.6, which showed the human income-expenditure balance for a non-monetary economy in which pure investment activity takes place.

2.4. The Income-Expenditure Balance for an Economy Including a Government Sector

We conclude this section by incorporating the third major entity in modern economic society—the government sector—into our model of a monetary economy. Here we assume that the government sector provides public goods and services, formulates economic stimulus measures and other policy objectives, and determines the level of government spending over a given period of time based on the total amount of income tax and corporate tax that it is able to collect from the household sector and corporate sector (respectively). Our definition of "government" can be understood to include local municipalities in addition to the national government.

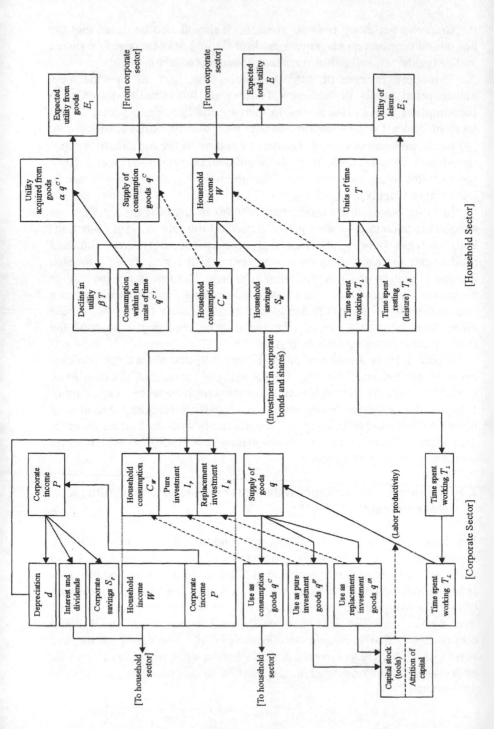

If the government maintains a balanced fiscal policy, then total government spending (G) will be equal to ($T_W + T_P$), or tax collected from the household sector (T_w) plus tax collected from the corporate sector (T_P). The government will then use G to purchase goods (q^G) from the corporate sector, which will then be used either for government consumption or public investment. Public investment activity contributes to the development of basic infrastructure such as housing, educational facilities, and public sewerage systems, industrial infrastructure such as roads, airports, and seaports, and other forms of public or social capital. In particular, public investment in industrial infrastructure is likely to improve the corporate sector's work productivity by improving the flow of goods (logistics) and making other positive contributions to production efficiency.

In cases where the private sector's pure investment (I_P) is lower than the combined savings of the household and corporate sectors ($S_W + S_P$), and where the necessary adjustments are slow to occur of their own accord, the government may temporarily abandon its emphasis on balanced fiscal policy with a view to maintaining a certain level of economic activity. It may do this by attempting to create new demand, funding its extra spending via issuance of government bonds designed to "soak up" excess savings within the household and corporate sectors, which would cause the government's debt to increase by D_G ($=S_W+S_P-I_P$). In this case, the government's total expenditure would be equal to ($T_W+T_P+D_G$), or income tax revenue (T_W) plus corporate tax revenue (T_P) plus the increase in government debt (D_G).

Figure 1.11 shows the income-expenditure balance for a government sector that raises funds from the household and corporate sectors in the form of income tax, corporate tax, and the proceeds of government bond issues (increases in its own debt), and spends this money on the provision of public goods and services as well as additions to the stock of public capital.

The household sector must pay part of its income (W) to the government in the form of income tax (T_W), while the corporate sector supplies part of its output to the government for use in the provision of public goods and services (q^G), and must pay part of its income (P) to the government in the form of corporate tax (T_P). Figure 1.12 incorporates these changes into the income-expenditure balances for the household and corporate sectors as shown in Figure 1.10, and then completes our framework by incorporating the income-expenditure balance for a government sector as shown in Figure 1.11.

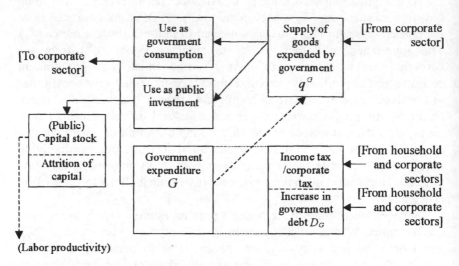

(Labor productivity)

Figure 1.11 "Income-expenditure balance for a government sector" in a monetary economy

3. The Fundamental Drivers of Demand

3.1. Implications of Our Analysis Based on the Income-Expenditure Balance

In Sections 1 and 2 of this chapter we constructed a "basic human accounting" framework that illustrates the interdependence of various "accounts"—utility, goods, time, and money—and has the following technical characteristics.

(1) Work time is the only input to our production function

Our analysis does not consider the capital stock to be a "fundamental" production factor, and is based on a production function that takes work (labor) time as its sole input (variable). We also make the simplifying assumption that the same level of productivity and the same production function apply to the production of consumption goods, investment goods, and goods to be expended by the government.

(2) Our analysis is based on long-term flows, and does not consider the impact of stock levels

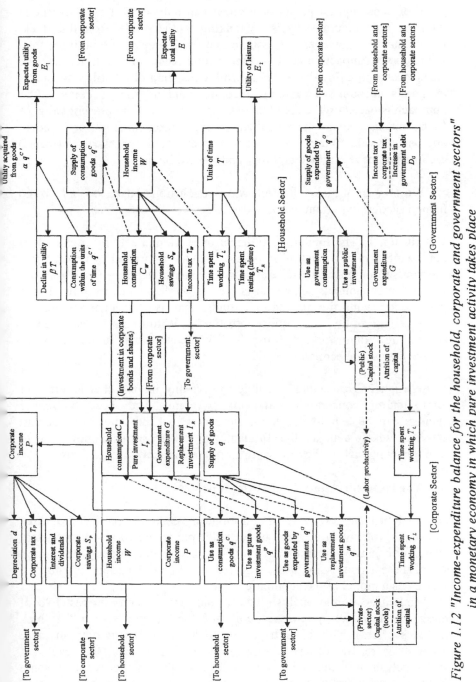

Figure 1.12 "Income-expenditure balance for the household, corporate and government sectors"
in a monetary economy in which pure investment activity takes place

People divide their time between work and leisure, and if they hold a stock of consumption goods or money, can reduce the time they spend working (on a temporary basis) by making "withdrawals" from this stock. In our analysis, however, we assume that stock levels have no more than a temporary impact, and that longer-term economic activity can be encapsulated in a flow-based framework consisting of a "utility account", a "goods account", a "money account", and a "time account". Our approach is based on the idea that asset values reflect the present value of future income flows (the so-called "capitalization method" or "income approach to value") and our belief that asset effects (or "wealth effects") are likely to have only a temporary and limited impact.

We may now make the following conclusions based on our "basic human accounting" framework.

Conclusion 1: The fundamental driver of economic activity (demand) is not the initial endowment of production factors (as argued by neoclassical economists) or pure investment or government spending (as argued by Keynesian economists); rather, it is the inevitable decline in utility levels that occurs with the passage of time (that is, the phenomenon of "diminishing utility" or "utility attrition"). Within our "basic human accounting" framework, it is the "utility account" that functions as the engine behind the economic cycle.

Conclusion 2: Households are able to save any income that is left over after funding consumption and tax payments, and these household savings can be lent to the corporate sector to fund "pure" investment activity, which acts as the fundamental driver of economic growth through its impact on the utility attrition rate and labor productivity.

3.2. The Need for Analysis of Human Desire

Our analytical framework for a non-monetary economy consisted of three "accounts" (utility, goods, and time), while our framework for a monetary economy consisted of four "accounts" (utility, goods, money, and time). All of these accounts are interconnected, and in combination they may be viewed as a model of the economic cycle.

Modern economic analysis has a tendency to focus on just two of these accounts, the "goods account" and the "money account" (which includes prices). This is perhaps due to the fact that activity in these accounts is readily observable or measurable. However, the results of such analysis will inevitably depart from reality in the event of some change to the underlying "utility account" (that is, a change in the level or nature of desire), and this is perhaps the key reason that modern economic analysis has been somewhat lacking in its ability to analyze (or explain) actual economic phenomena.

We would therefore argue that these limitations can only be overcome by constructing economic models that acknowledge the fundamental importance of human psychology by endogenizing the "utility account" (that is, the role of human desire). In our view, the development of such models should provide economists with a far greater capacity to analyze various economic phenomena such as the financial bubbles discussed at the start of this book.

NOTES

1. Defoe, D.(1719), *The Life and Strange Surprising Adventures of Robinson Crusoe*.
2. Say, J.B.(1836) argues in his *A Treatise on Political Economy* that "My reader... , so by consumption is meant the destruction of utility, and not of substance, or matter. When once the utility of a thing is destroyed, there is an end of the source and basis of its value; an extinction of that, which made it an object of desire and of demand. It thenceforward ceases to possess value, and is no longer an item of wealth." This concept is perhaps similar to the concept of "diminishing utility" that we present in this book.
3. Time spent consuming the consumption good (i.e. eating fish) should also be counted as leisure, but in order to simplify our analysis we assume that this time is so short that it can be ignored without affecting our conclusions.
4. We have used the word "expected" in relation to "total utility" because it includes "expected utility from goods" (E_1). This means that total utility is also determined as a stochastic average or mean.
5. As there are no banks or other institutions to act as intermediaries between the household and corporate sectors, we assume that firms raise funds by borrowing directly from households.

Chapter 2

Fundamentals of the Theory
of Diminishing Utility

In the previous chapter we outlined the basis for our theory of diminishing utility in the form of a "basic human accounting" framework that illustrates the interdependence of various "accounts"—utility, goods, (work) time, and money—for both a non-monetary and a monetary economy, and argued that diminishing utility is the fundamental driver of economic activity (demand). However, we have yet to discuss specific details of the "utility account", which functions as the engine of the economic cycle in our "basic human accounting" framework.

In this chapter we formalize the "utility account" by expressing the relationship between the passage of time and utility derived from goods in the form of a "utility attrition function" and clarifying the relationship between utility attrition (diminishing utility) and the psychology of desire. We then examine the relationships between the variables that constitute the utility account, and explain the fundamental concepts of "diminishing utility theory" that we shall use in the analysis that follows in subsequent chapters.

1. The Utility Attrition Function and a Model of Human Desire

1.1. The Utility Attrition Function and a Typical Example

Put simply, our concept of utility attrition (diminishing utility) is as follows: the energy derived from a single act of consumption inevitably diminishes with the passage of time (except in certain special cases). In other words, if we take "time" on the horizontal axis and "level of utility" on the vertical axis, then the (remaining) "level of utility" is described by a function that is downward sloping to the right. We refer to this function as the "utility attrition function", which we denote by $U(t)$. The idea that utility diminishes over time is captured by requiring that $dU / dt < 0$, and the utility attrition rate (the amount by which utility diminishes during a

31

very short period of time) may be defined as $-dU/dt$. For simplicity, we use $\beta(t)\{=-dU/dt\}$ to denote the utility attrition rate in our subsequent analysis. We also use α to denote the initial level of utility (energy) that is derived by consuming a single unit of the consumption good.

Figure 2.1 shows three different forms that the utility attrition function may take, together with the corresponding functions that describe the utility attrition rate. In each of (a), (b), and (c), the utility attrition function $U(t)$ is shown in the first quadrant, while the utility attrition rate function $\beta(t)$ is shown in the fourth quadrant.

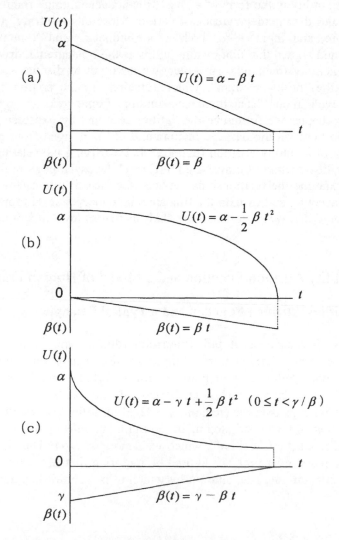

Figure 2.1 Typical forms of the utility attrition function

Example (a), in which $U(t) = \alpha - \beta t$ and $\beta(t) = \beta$ is consistent with our framework of Chapter 1 in that the utility attrition rate $\beta(t)$ remains constant over time. In this case, we refer to the utility attrition function— a straight line that is downward sloping to the right—as a "linear utility attrition function". This may be viewed as the most basic form of the utility attrition function, and is suitable for use in simplified economic models or when describing the steady state of an economy. It may also be useful for describing the remaining level of utility in relation to goods that are consumed at a fixed speed as part of human survival, such as food, water, and other consumable (expendable) goods.

Example (b), in which $U(t) = \alpha - (1/2)\beta t^2$ and $\beta(t) = \beta t$, shows a case in which the utility attrition rate $\beta(t)$ increases over time. In this case, we refer to the utility attrition function—a curve that is downward sloping to the right and concave with respect to the origin—as a "non-linear increasing-gradient utility attrition function". A function of this form may be useful in describing the remaining level of utility in relation to durable consumption goods and other physical (material) consumption goods that are designed for long-term use, as such products are typically designed so that the level of utility diminishes slowly during the initial period after the act of consumption.

Example (c), in which $U(t) = \alpha - \gamma t + (1/2)\beta t^2$ and $\beta(t) = \gamma - \beta t$, subject to $0 \leq t < \gamma / \beta$, shows a case in which the utility attrition rate $\beta(t)$ decreases over time. In this case, we refer to the utility attrition function—a curve that is downward sloping to the right and convex with respect to the origin—as a "non-linear decreasing-gradient utility attrition function". A function of this form describes a situation in which a larger proportion of utility is lost during the initial period after the act of consumption, and is similar in shape to the "Ebbinghaus retention curve" (or "forgetting curve"), which was first postulated by Hermann Ebbinghaus as a means of describing the amount of human memory that is retained with the passage of time. As such, a function of this form may be useful in describing the remaining level of utility in cases where this depends on the amount of retained memory.

We refer to (b) and (c) as examples of "non-linear utility attrition functions" due to the fact that the utility attrition rate changes over time. As noted earlier, example (a) describes a "linear utility attrition function" for which the utility attrition rate remains constant over time.

1.2. Special Examples of Utility Attrition Functions

For most goods (and services), the level of utility experienced by the consumer diminishes with the passage of time. However, there are certain goods for which the (remaining) level of utility $U(t)$ actually increases over time, or for which the initial level of utility α is maintained in perpetuity or for a given period of time (see Figure 2.2).

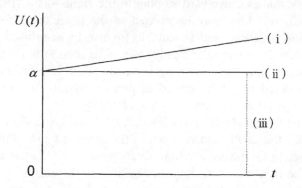

Figure 2.2 Special examples of utility attrition functions

Example (i) shows a case in which the (remaining) level of utility $U(t)$ increases over time. This may be the case for mementoes, memorabilia, antiques, and other goods that become more attractive with the passage of time, or goods for which the consumer may develop an attachment or sense of affection as a result of ongoing use.

Example (ii) shows a case in which the initial level of utility α is maintained in perpetuity. This may be the case for "goods" such as a tenured job position, permanent status, or a conferred title.

Example (iii) shows a case in which the initial level of utility α is maintained for a given period of time. Possible examples include a fixed-term sports club membership that entitles the owner to receive certain services for a specified period of time, or a bottle of shampoo or some other cosmetic product that contains multiple units of the consumption good and will provide the expected level of utility until the bottle is empty.

Examples (i) and (ii) could perhaps be handled by formulating a special utility attrition function with a negative or zero utility attrition rate, but we believe that there is no real benefit to be gained from considering such unusual cases, and have therefore decided to exclude them from the scope of our analysis.

Example (iii) must be incorporated into our analysis somehow, as it covers relatively common cases such as fixed-term service contracts and everyday consumables. One way of doing this is to replace the flat utility function with a linear utility attrition function that has the same integral over time (area under the curve) and a zero remaining utility balance upon conclusion of the contract period or consumption period. For example, if we denote the contract period in Example (iii) by t^c, then the area under the (flat) utility function is $\alpha\, t^c$. As can be seen from Figure 2.3, the linear utility attrition function described by $U(t) = 2\alpha\left[1 - (t / t^c)\right]$ (represented by the dotted line) has the same integral over time, and also satisfies the condition that $U(t^c) = 0$.

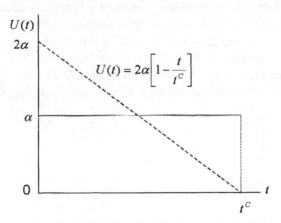

Figure 2.3 An example of artificially-imposed attrition

In other words, by replacing a flat utility function with an approximation that takes the form of a linear utility attrition function, it is possible to analyze the "exceptions" covered by Example (iii) as if they were "standard" goods or services for which the level of utility experienced by the consumer diminishes over time.

1.3. The Relationship Between Diminishing Utility and Human Desire

In this section we use the concept of a utility attrition function to examine the relationship between utility attrition (diminishing utility) and human desire.

As we have explained earlier in this book, all living beings must maintain a certain level of energy (on average) in order to survive. Let us now consider an example where Crusoe must maintain an average energy level (expected utility from goods) equal to E_1, obtains an initial utility level of α from consumption of a single fish, and sees this level of utility diminish over time as described by a linear utility attrition function of the form $U(t) = \alpha - \beta\, t$. In other words, Crusoe consumes energy at a constant speed of β (per unit time).

We first note that α (the initial level of utility) must exceed E_1 (the expected level of utility from goods). This is because the utility function is downward sloping to the right, which means that if the initial utility level is lower than the required utility level, then Crusoe will never be able to achieve the level of utility he requires in order to survive. If the initial level of utility is exactly equal to the expected level of utility (that is, if $\alpha = E_1$), then Crusoe will have to devote all his time to consumption in order to survive, and will have no time remaining for work or leisure, such that no more consumption goods will be produced.

We therefore assume that the initial utility level exceeds the required utility level (that is, $\alpha > E_1$), and show the relationship between the utility attrition function $U(t)$ and the expected utility level E_1 in Figure 2.4.

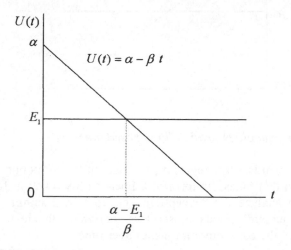

Figure 2.4 Relationship between the utility attrition function $U(t)$ and the expected utility level E_1

As can be seen from Figure 2.4, the remaining utility level $U(t)$ is greater than or equal to the expected utility level E_1 for $0 \leq t \leq (\alpha - E_1)/\beta$, which means that Crusoe experiences no sense of hunger during this time, and is able to devote his time to work (production of consumption goods), leisure, and other activities. In other words, Crusoe is free from desire relating to consumption goods (food) during this period of time.

However, once this threshold is passed, that is, $t > (\alpha - E_1)/\beta$, the level of utility experienced by Crusoe $U(t)$ is less than his expected utility level E_1. As a result, Crusoe begins to feel hunger and experience a desire for food (the consumption good). This desire becomes stronger the further that his actual level of utility falls below his expected level of utility. If Crusoe is unable to find a satisfactory source of food—such that this desire (hunger) continues to grow—then he will eventually move beyond physiological pain to a point where he is no longer able to survive.

In other words, the phenomenon of diminishing utility—which we have already identified as the fundamental driver of demand—only generates demand for new consumption goods when the consumer is experiencing a level of utility that is below his required level. This means that demand (desire) for new consumption goods arises in a discrete rather than a continuous manner. When a consumer is experiencing a level of utility from a consumption good that is above (or equal to) his required level, he is liberated from desire for that particular type of consumption good, and is therefore able to devote his time to work (production of consumption goods), leisure, and other activities (including consumption of other goods).

In summary, we may define "desire" in terms of the psychological need to alleviate—through the consumption of new consumption goods— the sense of psychological dissatisfaction or physical pain that arises as a result of a gap between one's expected (required) level of utility and one's actual level of utility. Such a gap may arise as a result of utility attrition or for some other reason.

We may now express the "desire function"—$w(t)$, which expresses the level of desire experienced by a consumer as a function of time—as follows:

$$w(t) = E_1 - U(t) \tag{2.1}$$

In the case of a linear utility attrition function given by $U(t) = \alpha - \beta\, t$, we obtain the following desire function:

$$w(t) = -(\alpha - E_1) + \beta\, t \tag{2.2}$$

The relationship between the remaining utility level $U(t)$, the expected utility level E_1, and the level of desire $w(t)$ is as shown in Figure 2.5.

As can be seen from Figure 2.5, if the linear utility attrition function remains unchanged while the expected utility level increases from E_1 to E_1', then the desire function $w(t)$ shifts up and to the left, such that the consumer experiences a greater level of desire at any given point of time.

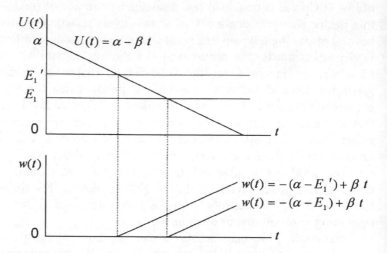

Figure 2.5 Relationship between the remaining utility level $U(t)$, the expected utility level E_1, and the level of desire $w(t)$

Conversely, if the expected utility level decreases from E_1' to E_1, then the desire function $w(t)$ shifts down and to the right, such that the consumer experiences a lower level of desire at any given point of time. This means that human desire—which arises as a result of utility attrition—can be controlled for a given period of time by adjusting one's own expectations. For example, if a person feels that he may find it difficult to obtain consumption goods due to a decline in income or some other adverse circumstances, then he may try to minimize his feeling of desire for certain types of consumption goods by lowering his expected (desired) level of utility (E_1) from those goods. However, expectations can only be adjusted to a limited extent in the case of necessities (such as food) that satisfy physiological needs. In other words, the more necessary a given consumption good, the more difficult it is to control desire relating to that good; conversely, the less necessary a given consumption good (i.e. the more that it may be characterized as a luxury item), the easier it is to control desire relating to that good.

1.4. A Consideration of Consumption Units

As we discussed in the previous section, it is essential for α (the initial level of utility from a consumption good) to exceed E_1 (the expected level of utility from that good). This means that we must consider two different cases with regard to the units in which goods are available for purchase: (1) the case where consumption of a single unit yields an initial level of utility that is higher than the expected level of utility (for example, a durable consumption good such as a car); and (2) the case where multiple units must be purchased in order to experience an initial level of utility that is higher than the expected level of utility (for example, a case where a person must eat two bread rolls and drink a bottle of milk in order to alleviate his hunger). In the second case, purchase of a single unit would leave the consumer dissatisfied in that his desire would remain unfulfilled. In other words, the consumer is unable to (temporarily) overcome his desire unless he consumes multiple units of the consumption good, thereby achieving an initial level of utility that is higher than his expected level of utility.

Given that the desire to be fulfilled is the same (for example, elimination of hunger pains), it seems fair to treat consumption of multiple units of one or more consumption goods as a single act of consumption. In other words, we may treat such a set of consumption goods as a single "composite consumption good" that costs the same as the sum of the prices of the constituent goods. So long as the desire to be satisfied is the same, it should be possible to handle standard consumption goods and composite consumption goods in identical fashion.

Let us now consider a simple example of a composite consumption good. Suppose that I go to a bar with a budget of $25 and consume three "units" of beer and two "units" of peanuts—each of which costs $5—and experience a sense of satisfaction. In this case, my goal is that of alleviating stress, and this objective is achieved through the purchase of a "set" of consumption goods consisting of three glasses of beer and two packets of nuts. It therefore seems appropriate to analyze this behavior in terms of a single act of consumption of a composite consumption good (costing $25) rather than focusing on the level of utility that is attained through consumption of each of the individual goods.

2. Modeling the "Utility Account" and Derivation of the Goods Utility Function

In the previous section we formalized the concept of "desire" based on the utility attrition function and the expected level of utility (from goods), treating the average level of utility (energy) that must be maintained by the consumer as an exogenous variable.

In this section we formalize the "utility account"—which functions as the engine of the economic cycle in our "basic human accounting" framework—by deriving the "goods utility function", which describes the relationship between the amount consumed during a given period of time

(q^c) and the expected level of utility from goods (E_1). Note that the following discussion assumes a linear utility attrition function.

2.1. Modeling the "Utility Account" and Derivation of the Goods Utility Function

We begin by revisiting the "utility account" in our "basic human accounting" framework (see Figure 2.6 below). We assume that the utility attrition rate remains constant over time (i.e. $\beta(t)=\beta$), such that the (linear) utility attrition function takes the form $U(t) = \alpha - \beta\, t$.

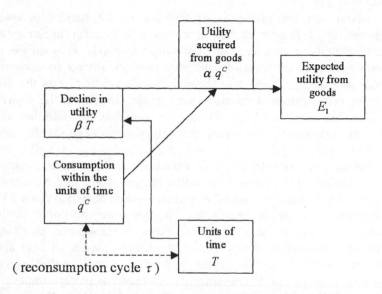

Figure 2.6 Causal relationship between variables related to diminishing utility

As we discussed in the previous section, the phenomenon of diminishing utility means that demand (desire) for new consumption goods arises in a discrete rather than a continuous manner. If q^c acts of consumption take place within T units of time (as shown in Figure 2.6), then the average time from one act of consumption to the next can be expressed as T/q^c. We refer to this average time as the "reconsumption cycle", which we denote by τ. In other words:

$$\tau = \frac{T}{q^c} \tag{2.3}$$

We also make the following two assumptions for the purpose of our analysis.

First, we assume that (only) a single consumption good is used for a single consumption goal or objective, which means that if a consumption good is renewed as a result of reconsumption, only the renewed consumption good is used by the consumer (with the pre-renewal consumption goods no longer being used for a consumption goal or objective, or ceasing to exist). This assumption ensures that the outstanding utility balance associated with the previous act of consumption is not added to the (new) utility balance associated with the current act of consumption, and is appropriate for modeling the replacement of cars and other consumption goods for which a single unit is sufficient for any given household (or individual).

Second, we assume that reconsumption (the next act of consumption) occurs before the balance of utility derived from the previous act of consumption has fallen to zero (that is, we assume $\tau < \alpha/\beta$). This means that a consumer does not completely "use up" or "exhaust" a consumption good before purchasing the next consumption good, such that a certain amount of remaining utility goes to waste. This assumption would appear to be consistent with the consumption behavior that is typically observed in real life.

Figure 2.7 shows the linear utility attrition function based on the above assumptions, assuming that consumption takes place in regular intervals with a "reconsumption cycle" of τ.

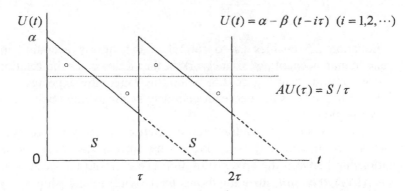

Figure 2.7 Relationship between "reconsumption cycle" of τ and average level of utility $AU(\tau)$

As can be seen from Figure 2.7, the consumer's level of utility initially takes the value α as a result of consumption at time $t=0$, and then diminishes over time before rising back to α as a result of consumption at time $t = \tau$. This cycle is repeated over time with a frequency of τ, such that the consumer's level of utility follows a sawtooth pattern. If we denote the average level of utility with a "reconsumption cycle" of τ by $AU(\tau)$, then $AU(\tau)$ is equal to the level shown in Figure 2.7, where the circles denote areas of equal magnitude.

This average level of utility can be calculated by dividing the area bounded by the linear utility attrition function $U(t)$ and the horizontal axis over the interval $0 \le t \le \tau$ (denoted by S in Figure 2.7) by the "reconsumption cycle" τ. S can be calculated as follows:

$$S = \int_0^\tau U(t)dt = \int_0^\tau (\alpha - \beta\, t)dt = \alpha\tau - \frac{1}{2}\beta\tau^2$$

which means that the average level of utility is given by:

$$AU(\tau) = \frac{S}{\tau} = \alpha - \frac{1}{2}\beta\tau \qquad (2.4)$$

We may then eliminate τ from Equations (2.3) and (2.4) to obtain the goods utility function, which describes the average level of utility experienced by a consumer given that q^c units of the consumption good are consumed within T units of time:

$$AU(q^c) = \alpha - \frac{1}{2}\frac{\beta T}{q^c} \qquad (2.5)$$

Equation 2.5 enables us to formalize the "utility account" in our "basic human accounting" framework in that it describes the relationship between q^c and E_1 in Figure 2.6, where the latter (the expected level of utility from goods) is derived endogenously as the average balance of the utility function, $AU(q^c)$.

Figure 2.8 is a four-quadrant representation of $AU(q^c)$ along with the functions from which it is derived. The second quadrant shows the relationship between the "reconsumption cycle" τ and the average utility level $AU(\tau)$, the third quadrant shows the (trivial) relationship $\tau = \tau$, the fourth quadrant shows the relationship between the "reconsumption cycle" τ *and* q^c (the quantity consumed within T units of time), and the first quadrant shows the goods utility function $AU(q^c)$ based on the functions shown in the other three quadrants.

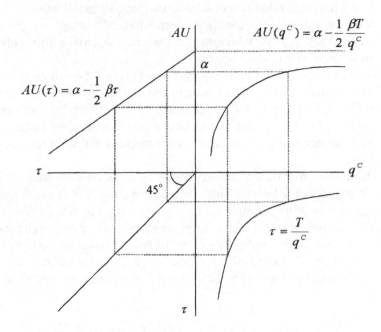

$$AU(q^c) = \alpha - \frac{1}{2}\frac{\beta T}{q^c}$$

$$AU(\tau) = \alpha - \frac{1}{2}\beta\tau$$

$$\tau = \frac{T}{q^c}$$

Figure 2.8 Derivation of the goods utility function $AU(q^c)$ under a four-quadrant representation

2.2. Attributes of the Goods Utility Function

As can be seen from Equation 2.5, the goods utility function $AU(q^c)$ is a convex hyperbola with respect to the coordinates $(q^c, AU) = (0, \alpha)$, and is an increasing function in q^c (the quantity consumed within T units of time). The first and second derivatives of $AU(q^c)$ are given by $dAU/dq^c = \beta T/2(q^c)^2 > 0$ and $d^2AU/d(q^c)^2 = -\beta T/(q^c)^3 < 0$, respectively, which means that the goods utility function satisfies the principle of diminishing marginal utility.

Other properties of the goods utility function $AU(q^c)$ are as follows:

(1) The curve has no kinks and is everywhere-differentiable.
(2) There is no saturation point, i.e. no point where dAU/dq^c equals zero.
(3) $q^c > 0$ when $AU(q^c)=0$.

With regard to (1), q^c does not represent the amount of consumption that is actually observed during T units of time, but instead represents the value obtained by dividing the T units of time by the "reconsumption cycle" τ. This means that q^c can take infinitesimally small values.

With regard to (2), the first derivative of $AU(q^c)$ is given by $dAU / dq^c = \beta T / 2(q^c)^2$, which means that the marginal utility only falls to zero when q^c is infinitely large.

With regard to (3), it can be seen from Figure 2.6—which shows the "utility account" for our "basic human accounting" framework—that the amount of utility derived from goods (αq^c) is offset by the (natural) decline in utility (βT). This means that a positive level of consumption (q^c) will be necessary in order to achieve (net) utility from goods of $AU(q^c)=0$.[1]

The above properties of the goods utility function were derived under the assumption of a linear utility attrition function, but it can be shown that the goods utility function has the same properties if the utility attrition function is non-linear in form, as shown in Figure 2.1 (b) and (c).

In the case of Example (b)—a "non-linear increasing-gradient utility attrition function" described by $U(t) = \alpha - (1/2)\beta\, t^2$—we may calculate $AU(\tau)$, the average level of utility with a "reconsumption cycle" of τ, as follows:

$$S = \int_0^\tau U(t)dt = \int_0^\tau \{\alpha - (1/2)\beta\, t^2\}dt = \alpha\tau - \frac{1}{6}\beta\tau^3$$

$$AU(\tau) = \frac{S}{\tau} = \alpha - \frac{1}{6}\beta\tau^2 \tag{2.6}$$

Eliminating τ from Equations (2.3) and (2.6) yields the goods utility function:

$$AU(q^c) = \alpha - \frac{1}{6}\frac{\beta T^2}{(q^c)^2} \tag{2.7}$$

The first and second derivatives of $AU(q^c)$ are given by $dAU / dq^c = \beta T^2 / 3(q^c)^3 > 0$ and $d^2 AU / d(q^c)^2 = -\beta T^2 /(q^c)^4 < 0$, respectively, which means that the goods utility function satisfies the principle of diminishing marginal utility, and has the three properties listed above [(1)–(3)].

Similarly, in the case of Example (c)—a "non-linear decreasing-gradient utility attrition function" described by $U(t) = \alpha - \gamma\, t + (1/2)\,\beta\, t^2$, defined on domain $0 \le t < \gamma / \beta$—we may calculate $AU(\tau)$, the average level of utility with a "reconsumption cycle" of τ, as follows:

$$S = \int_0^\tau U(t)dt = \int_0^\tau \left\{\alpha - \gamma\, t + (1/2)\,\beta\, t^2\right\}dt = \alpha\tau - \frac{1}{2}\,\gamma\,\tau^2 + \frac{1}{6}\beta\tau^3$$

$$AU(\tau) = \frac{S}{\tau} = \alpha - \frac{1}{2}\,\gamma\,\tau + \frac{1}{6}\beta\tau^2 \tag{2.8}$$

Eliminating τ from Equations (2.3) and (2.8) yields the goods utility function:[2]

$$AU(q^c) = \alpha - \frac{\gamma\,T}{2q^c} + \frac{1}{6}\frac{\beta T^2}{(q^c)^2} \tag{2.9}$$

where $q^c > \beta T/\gamma$

The first and second derivatives of $AU(q^c)$ are given by $dAU/dq^c = T/(q^c)^3 \{(\gamma/2)q^c - (\beta T/3)\}$ and $d^2AU/d(q^c)^2 = -T/(q^c)^4(\gamma\, q^c - \beta T)$, respectively. On the domain $q^c > \beta T/\gamma$, the first derivative is positive while the second derivative is negative, which means that the goods utility function satisfies the principle of diminishing marginal utility, and has the first two properties listed above [(1)–(2)]. Property (3) applies only if $\gamma > (3\alpha\beta)^{1/2}$.

2.3. Changes in the Utility Attrition Rate and Their Impact on Demand

In this section we consider how changes in the utility attrition rate affect the shape of the goods utility function and the level of demand for the consumption good.

Figure 2.9 is a four-quadrant representation of the goods utility function $AU(q^c)$ and the functions from which it is derived for the case of a linear utility attrition function. The current utility attrition rate is represented by β_0 (>0), and the goods utility function $AU(q^c)$ and the average utility level function $AU(\tau)$ that correspond to this utility attrition rate are denoted by the solid lines labeled (i) in the first and second quadrants.

Let us now assume that the utility attrition rate increases to β_1 (>β_0), such that the slope ($\beta/2$) of the average utility level function $AU(\tau)$ shown in the second quadrant increases, producing the steeper straight (dotted) line labeled (ii) in the second quadrant. This would cause the goods utility function $AU(q^c)$ shown in the first quadrant to shift downwards and to the right (from (i) to (ii) as shown), which means that an increase in the utility attrition rate leads to a lower average level of utility for a given rate of consumption (q^c).

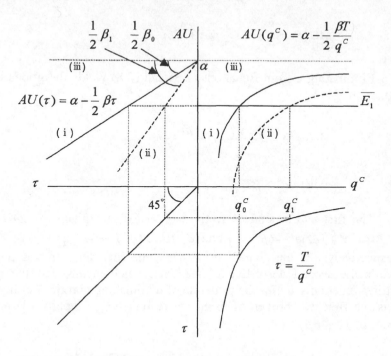

Figure 2.9 Relationship between change in the utility attrition rate and that in the demand of goods

Conversely, a decrease in the utility attrition rate would cause the slope of the average utility level function $AU(\tau)$ shown in the second quadrant to decrease and the goods utility function $AU(q^c)$ shown in the first quadrant to shift upwards and to the left, which means that a decrease in the utility attrition rate leads to a higher average level of utility for a given rate of consumption (q^c).

If the utility attrition rate is zero, such that utility does not diminish over time, then the average utility level function $AU(\tau)$ takes the form shown by the flat dotted line labeled (iii) in the second quadrant, and the goods utility function $AU(q^c)$ is also a flat straight line (shown as (iii) in the first quadrant). In other words, in the case of a consumption good for which utility does not diminish over time, the initial level of utility (α) is maintained in perpetuity, such that the length of the "reconsumption cycle" (τ) and the rate of consumption (q^c) have no impact on the level of utility experienced by the consumer in relation to the consumption good in question.

We next consider a case where the level of utility (energy) that must be maintained on average by the consumer (the expected utility from goods, or E_1) is an endogenous variable $\overline{E_1}$ as shown in the first quadrant in Figure 2.9, and once again consider the impact of a change in the utility attrition rate on the level of demand.

If the utility attrition rate increases from β_0 to β_1 ($>\beta_0$), then the goods utility function $AU(q^c)$ shifts downwards and to the right (from (i) to (ii) as shown in the first quadrant), such that the rate of consumption necessary in order to maintain the expected level of utility increases from ($q_0{}^c$) to ($q_1{}^c$). The actual level of q^c can be expressed as follows by using $AU(q^c) = \overline{E_1}$ to eliminate $AU(q^c)$ from Equation (2.5):

$$q^c = \frac{\beta T}{2(\alpha - \overline{E_1})} \tag{2.10}$$

This shows that for a given expected utility level, an increase in the utility attrition rate serves to increase the rate of consumption (q^c) in any given period of time, while a decrease in the utility attrition rate serves to decrease the rate of consumption.

2.4. The Goods Utility Function Under Relaxed Assumptions

In deriving the goods utility function earlier in this chapter (in Section 2.1), we assumed that (only) a single consumption good is used for a single consumption goal or objective, such that the outstanding utility balance associated with the previous act of consumption is not added to the (new) utility balance associated with the current act of consumption. Based on this assumption, we derived the goods utility function $AU(q^c)$, which is an increasing function in q^c that satisfies the principle of diminishing marginal utility.

In this section we once again assume a linear utility attrition function, and derive the goods utility function under a scenario where utility can be accumulated over time (that is, where utility from a new act of consumption can be added to the existing level of utility derived from previous acts of consumption). By considering the shape and properties of the goods utility function derived under this scenario, we illustrate the significance of our assumption regarding non-accumulation of utility across acts of consumption.

We retain the second assumption made in Section 2.1, i.e. that reconsumption (the next act of consumption) occurs before the balance of utility derived from the previous act of consumption has fallen to zero (that is, we assume $\tau < \alpha/\beta$), but now allow the utility remaining after the end of a "reconsumption cycle" (that is, over the period defined by $\tau < t \le \alpha/\beta$) to be added to the utility derived from the next act of consumption. This results in "bent" linear utility attrition functions as shown in Figure 2.10.

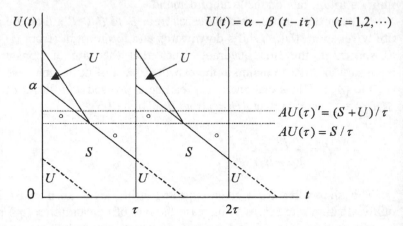

Figure 2.10 Relationship between "reconsumption cycle" of τ and average level of utility $AU(\tau)'$ under relaxed assumptions

The average utility level function under the assumption that utility can be accumulated across acts of consumption—which we shall denote by $AU(\tau)'$—can be derived as follows based on the areas S (the area under the linear utility attrition function $U(t)$ on the domain $0 \le t \le \tau$) and U (the area under the linear utility attrition function $U(t)$ on the domain $\tau < t \le \alpha/\beta$) that are shown in Figure 2.10:

$$S = \int_0^\tau U(t)dt = \int_0^\tau (\alpha - \beta t)dt = \alpha\tau - \frac{1}{2}\beta\tau^2$$

$$U = \int_\tau^{\alpha/\beta} U(t)dt = \int_\tau^{\alpha/\beta} (\alpha - \beta t)dt = \frac{1}{2}\frac{\alpha^2}{\beta} - (\alpha\tau - \frac{1}{2}\beta\tau^2)$$

$$AU(\tau)' = \frac{S+U}{\tau} = \frac{1}{2}\frac{\alpha^2}{\beta}\frac{1}{\tau} \qquad (2.11)$$

Eliminating τ from Equations (2.3) and (2.11) yields the goods utility function:

$$AU(q^c)' = \frac{1}{2}\frac{\alpha^2}{\beta T}q^c \qquad (2.12)$$

This goods utility function is the linear function shown in Figure 2.11, which has (constant) marginal utility given by $dAU'/dq^c = (1/2)\alpha^2/\beta T$.

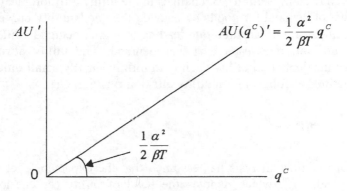

Figure 2.11 Goods utility function under relaxed assumptions

Unfortunately, however, this linear goods utility function is unacceptable for the following two reasons.

First, it is unreasonable to assume that a consumption good has a constant rate of marginal utility. As is well known, the law of demand (which implies a demand curve that is a decreasing function of price) is premised on the principle of diminishing marginal utility.

Second, use of the linear goods utility function (2.12) would mean that α—the initial level of utility derived from an act of consumption—would be included in the set of explanatory variables for the equilibrium levels of employment, output, and other key variables. This is inappropriate, as it would require the absolute level of utility (α) to be measurable and comparable across persons, which is impossible as a matter of practice (as argued by Lionel C. Robbins). For this reason, we have excluded linear goods utility functions from our analysis.[3]

The above discussion shows that allowing utility to be added across different acts of consumption may result in an unrealistic goods utility function, and may also make our analysis unnecessarily complicated. It is for this reason that our analysis is based on the assumption that (only) a single consumption good is used for a single consumption goal or objective, such that the outstanding utility balance associated with the previous act of consumption is not added to the (new) utility balance associated with the current act of consumption.

3. An Extension of the Concept of Diminishing Utility and Factors that Determine the Utility Attrition Rate

3.1. The Relativity of Utility Attrition Rate Determination

As we showed in Section 2.3, changes to the utility attrition rate (β) affect the level of demand for goods by causing the goods utility curve to shift, with a higher utility attrition rate leading to higher demand while a lower utility attrition rate leads to lower demand. The utility attrition rate denotes the decline in utility during an infinitesimally small unit of time, as is defined as follows for a utility attrition function $U(t)$:

$$\beta(t) = -\frac{dU(t)}{dt} \tag{2.13}$$

Our previous analysis has assumed that the expected level of utility from goods—E_1, which denotes the level of utility (or energy) that a consumer hopes or needs to achieve—remains constant over time, such that the utility attrition rate is determined in an absolute sense based on the slope of the utility attrition function.

However, given that the expected level of utility from goods (E_1) is dependent on human psychology, there is no need for it to remain constant over time; indeed, it may be more natural to assume that E_1 is likely to fluctuate as a result of a consumer's changing expectations regarding the future. In this section we examine how the utility attrition function is determined under a scenario where the expected level of utility from goods (E_1) changes over time.

We begin by examining a case where the expected level of utility from goods at the time of consumption ($t=0$) is E_1^0, and where this level increases at a constant rate (β_2) over the period from $t=0$ to $t=t_0$ and then remains constant for $t \geq t_0$. The utility attrition function in this example (shown in the first quadrant of Figure 2.12) has the linear form $U(t) = \alpha - \beta_1 t$.

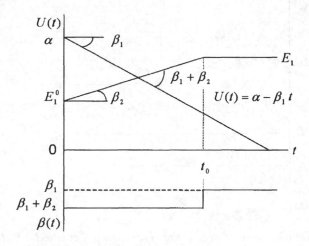

Figure 2.12 Relationship between the increasing expected utility from goods (E_1) and the generalized (relative) utility attrition rate

As can be seen from Figure 2.12, the expected level of utility from goods (E_1) increases at a rate of $dE_1/dt = \beta_2$ between the time of consumption and $t=t_0$, such that the consumer's *subjective* utility attrition rate is higher (by β_2) than it would be if the consumer's expected level of utility were not increasing over time. In other words, even if the consumption good's utility attrition rate remains unchanged, changes to the expected level of utility—another subjective criterion—serve to exacerbate or mitigate the impact of utility attrition. This means that the utility attrition rate is determined in a *relative* fashion that depends on changes to the expected level of utility. As such, the utility attrition rate $\beta(t)$ is equal to $\beta_1+\beta_2$ for $0 \leq t < t_0$ and equal to β_1 for $t_0 \leq t$ (as shown in the fourth quadrant in Figure 2.12).

The first quadrant of Figure 2.13 shows the case where the expected level of utility from goods (E_1) *decreases* at a constant rate (β_2) over the period from $t=0$ to $t=t_0$ and then remains constant for $t \geq t_0$.

As can be seen from Figure 2.13, the expected level of utility from goods (E_1) decreases at a rate of $dE_1/dt = \beta_2$ between the time of consumption and $t=t_0$, such that the consumer's *subjective* utility attrition rate is lower (by β_2) than it would be if the consumer's expected level of utility were not decreasing over time. As such, the utility attrition rate $\beta(t)$ is equal to $\beta_1-\beta_2$ for $0 \leq t < t_0$ and equal to β_1 for $t_0 \leq t$ (as shown in the fourth quadrant in Figure 2.13).

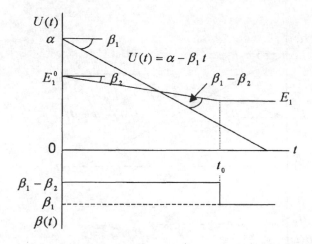

Figure 2.13 Relationship between the decreasing expected utility from goods (E_1) and the generalized (relative) utility attrition rate

The generalized (relative) utility attrition rate for cases where the expected level of utility from goods—E_1, which denotes the level of utility (or energy) that a consumer hopes or needs to achieve—changes over time can be defined as follows:

$$\beta(t) = -\frac{dU(t)}{dt} + \frac{dE_1}{dt} \qquad (2.14)$$

Equation (2.14) can be used to ensure that the utility attrition rate reflects special circumstances, such as in the following examples.

1. An example where the absolute utility attrition rate (based on the utility attrition function) is positive, but the generalized utility attrition rate is zero:
 If we set $\beta(t)$ to zero in Equation (2.14), then we obtain $-dE_1/dt = -dU(t)/dt$. In the case of a linear utility function of form $U(t) = \alpha - \beta t$, $-dU(t)/dt = \beta$, such that $-dE_1/dt = \beta$. This corresponds to the case where the expected level of utility from goods (E_1) decreases at the same rate as the level of utility $U(t)$, such that the generalized utility attrition rate is zero over the period in question despite the absolute utility attrition rate being positive.

2. An example where the absolute utility attrition rate (based on the utility attrition function) is zero, but the generalized utility attrition rate is positive:

If we set $-dU(t)/dt$ to zero in Equation (2.14), then we obtain $\beta(t) = dE_1 / dt$. This corresponds to a good for which the consumer initially has a zero expected level of utility (i.e. an undesired good), such that the consumer does not consume the good and both the utility level $U(t)$ and the utility attrition rate $-dU(t)/dt$ are zero. If the expected level of utility from this good (E_1) increases over time due to the launch of a new model or the addition of new functionality based on corporate investment, an increase in real income (due to an increase in the expected level of future income or a decrease in the price of the good, including subjective expectations), an external effect such as consumption by other people, or due to some other factor that serves to make the good more desirable, then the generalized utility attrition rate will be equal to dE_1 / dt (the rate at which the expected or required level of utility is increasing).

3.2. The Impact of Goods Maintenance and Damage

In addition to changes in the expected level of utility (E_1), the generalized utility attrition rate may also be affected by departures of the utility attrition function from its initial schedule, which could arise as a result of maintenance of a good or damage to a good. Here we use the word "maintenance" to describe any act that serves to slow the pace at which a good loses functionality, such as the expenditure of money or effort to prolong the period for which the good remains in satisfactory condition, and use the word "damage" to describe any factor that serves to accelerate the pace at which a good loses functionality, including external factors such as war, disaster, or accident and "internal" factors such as excessive use by the consumer or use in a harsh environment.

Figure 2.14 shows an example where the expected level of utility (E_1) remains unchanged, the utility attrition function has the linear form $U(t) = \alpha - \beta_1 t$, and the good is "maintained" on an ongoing basis from $t=t_0$ onwards.

Figure 2.15 shows an example where the expected level of utility (E_1) remains unchanged, the utility attrition function has the linear form $U(t) = \alpha - \beta_1 t$, and the good suffers continual damage from $t=t_0$ onwards.

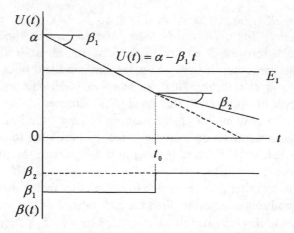

Figure 2.14 Impact of goods maintenance on the utility attrition rate

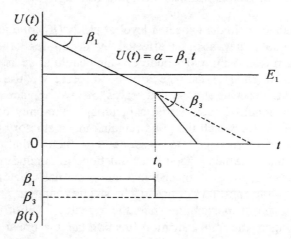

Figure 2.15 Impact of damage on the utility attrition rate

As can be seen from Figures 2.14 and 2.15, the utility attrition rate remains constant (at β_1) between the time of consumption and $t=t_0$, and then decreases to β_2 ($<\beta_1$) in the case where the good is maintained, or increases to β_3 ($>\beta_1$) in the case where the good suffers continual damage.

In the case of an external factor such as war, disaster, or accident, the level of utility may (in many cases) instantaneously fall to zero at time $t=t_0$, corresponding to an infinitely high utility attrition rate (an infinitely high level of desire). This would produce a sharp increase in the level of demand for goods similar to the demand surge that typically follows a war or major calamity.

3.3. Utility Attrition and Its Causes

The utility attrition function describes the level of subjective utility experienced by a consumer as a result of consumption of a particular good. Our analysis is not limited to consumption of food for the purpose of survival (the acquisition of an initial level of utility followed by internal consumption of energy, as discussed in Chapter 1), and the utility attrition function can be viewed more generally as describing the inevitable (in most cases) loss of the subjective value that a person derives from a single act of consumption. Factors that contribute to this loss of subjective value—or attrition of utility—can perhaps be categorized as follows.

(1) Attrition over time [typically a natural attrition as a result of the passage of time]
   - Internal consumption of energy and water for the purpose of survival (e.g. food, water)
   - Loss of affection / attachment due to something going out of fashion (e.g. clothes and other fashion items)
   - Decline in quality with age (e.g. fading of products in sunlight)
(2) Attrition with use [typically attrition as a result of a good's use by the consumer]
   - Loss of functionality due to wear and tear (e.g. shoes, tires, and other consumable items)
   - Loss of functionality due to breakdown (e.g. cars and other durable consumer items)
   - Loss of interest due to repeated use (e.g. game software)
(3) Artificially-imposed attrition [attrition after a certain level of utility has been maintained for a given period]
   - Fixed-term services (e.g. sports club memberships)
   - Goods for which a single purchase unit includes a sufficient quantity for multiple acts of consumption (e.g. detergent, cosmetics, etc.)

We now summarize the interaction between these factors and their role in determining the utility attrition rate (the speed with which desire grows), taking into account our discussion of "relativity" in Section 3.1 of this chapter.

Factors contributing to the utility attrition rate

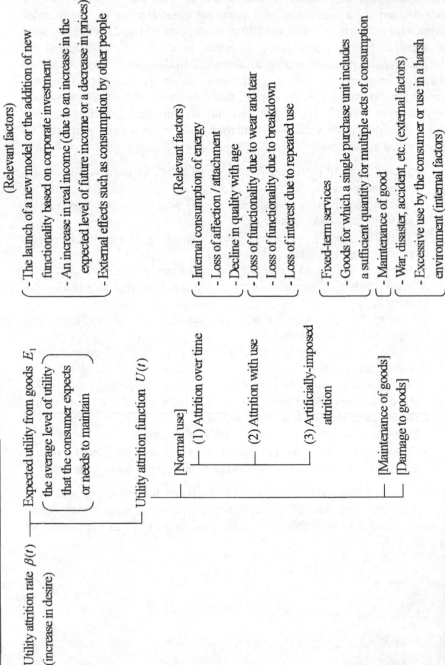

Utility attrition rate $\beta(t)$ (increase in desire) — Expected utility from goods E_1 (the average level of utility that the consumer expects or needs to maintain)

(Relevant factors)
- The launch of a new model or the addition of new functionality based on corporate investment
- An increase in real income (due to an increase in the expected level of future income or a decrease in prices)
- External effects such as consumption by other people

Utility attrition function $U(t)$

[Normal use]

(1) Attrition over time

(2) Attrition with use

(3) Artificially-imposed attrition

(Relevant factors)
- Internal consumption of energy
- Loss of affection / attachment
- Decline in quality with age

- Loss of functionality due to wear and tear
- Loss of functionality due to breakdown
- Loss of interest due to repeated use

- Fixed-term services
- Goods for which a single purchase unit includes a sufficient quantity for multiple acts of consumption

[Maintenance of goods]
[Damage to goods]

- Maintenance of good
- War, disaster, accident, etc. (external factors)
- Excessive use by the consumer or use in a harsh environment (internal factors)

Except in the case of maintenance of goods, the factors shown on p. 56 are those that contribute to an increase in the utility attrition rate (the speed at which desire grows), such that a decline in such factors—or an occurrence of the opposite phenomenon—acts to reduce the utility attrition rate (the speed at which desire grows).

3.4. Real Utility Attrition and Monetary Utility Attrition

Factors contributing to the generalized (relative or subjective) utility attrition rate defined in Equation (2.14) can be categorized either as: (1) the desire—habitual or new—to purchase a product for consumption based on the consumer's assessment of its functionality and suitability; and (2) a spontaneous desire to purchase a number of unspecified goods, primarily as a result of an increase in buying power due to monetary factors. In this book we draw a clear distinction between these two types of factors, classifying the former as "real utility attrition" and the latter as "monetary utility attrition". The following table summarizes factors that are relevant to the generalized utility attrition rate defined in Equation (2.14) and shows whether they represent "real utility attrition" or "monetary utility attrition".

Generalized (relative or subjective) utility attrition rate		Relevant factors	Type of utility attrition
$\beta(t)$	$-\dfrac{dU(t)}{dt}$	The utility attrition function $U(t)$ for the consumption good	Real utility attrition
	$\dfrac{dE_1}{dt}$	The launch of a new model or the addition of new functionality based on corporate investment	
		External effects such as consumption by other people (demonstration effects, etc.)	
		An increase in real income (due to an increase in the expected level of future income or a decrease in prices)	Monetary utility attrition

Table 2.1 Relevant factors of the generalized utility attrition rate and the type of utility attrition

Based on the above classification, we may define the generalized utility attrition rate as the sum of the "real utility attrition" rate and the "monetary utility attrition" rate. In Sections 1.2 and 1.3 of Chapter 5 of this book, we consider the interaction of "real" and "monetary" utility attrition factors and analyze the impact of monetary factors on the economic cycle as well as the process by which economic bubbles are formed and destroyed.

NOTES

1. For the case where consumption occurs at the start of a period of T units of time, utility diminishes for a period of T units of time; where consumption occurs at the end of the period, utility diminishes for a period of zero units of time. On average, utility diminishes for a period of $(T+0)/2 = T/2$ units of times, such that the consumer's utility diminishes by $\beta T/2$. When $AU(q^c)=0$, $\beta T/2$ is equal to αq^c, such that $q^c = \beta T/2\alpha$ (>0).

2. The "reconsumption cycle" τ is defined over the domain $0 \le \tau < \gamma/\beta$. Substituting $\tau = T/q^c$ and rearranging yields $q^c > \beta T/\gamma$.

3. This does not preclude discussion of the possibility that α (the initial level of utility) and β (the utility attrition rate) may be correlated. For example, it is possible that α could be proportional to β in the case of goods with a fixed useful life. However, such cases can easily be modeled through the utility attrition rate β.

Chapter 3

Analysis of a Non-Monetary Economy

In this chapter we use "The Human Income-Expenditure Balance in a Non-Monetary (Robinson Crusoe) Economy" (Figure 1.6 of Chapter 1, Section 1) to construct a theoretical framework in which output and the allocation of resources are simultaneously determined as a result of the process whereby a person maximizes expected total utility (the sum of expected utility from goods and utility of leisure) against a backdrop of diminishing utility, and derive the "basic equation of labor" for a non-monetary economy.

Assumptions Behind Our Analysis

The analysis in this chapter is based on the following simplifying assumptions:

(1) In cases where Crusoe consumes a number of consumption goods on an ongoing basis, the utility associated with a given consumption good depends solely on the amount of that good consumed by Crusoe, i.e. it does not depend on the amounts of other consumption goods consumed by Crusoe.

(2) Expected utility E_1 (a measure of the satisfaction derived by Crusoe from consumption of a given good) is not affected by time spent resting (T_R), nor is utility from leisure E_2 (a measure of the satisfaction derived by Crusoe from time taken to restore productive capacity) affected by time spent working (T_L). In other words, expected utility E_1 depends solely on time spent working (T_L), and utility from leisure E_2 depends solely on time spent resting (T_R).

(3) As consumer, Crusoe consumes two different consumption goods (Good 1 and Good 2), while as producer, Crusoe produces two different consumption goods (Good 1 and Good 2) and one pure investment good (Good 3).

(4) Crusoe's utility attrition function for each consumption good is linear (that is, each consumption good has a constant utility attrition rate).

(5) A capital stock exists at the start of the analysis period, and the capital attrition rate is zero. In terms of Figure 1.6, this means that the proportion allocated to capital is zero, and there is no flow of "replacement investment". In other words, all output is allocated to Crusoe.

(6) Pure investment during the analysis period does not add to the capital stock, and has no impact on utility attrition rates or labor productivity during the analysis period.

Assumptions (1) and (2) ensure additivity of utility, such that in cases where Crusoe consumes a number of consumption goods on an ongoing basis, expected utility from these goods E_1 can be calculated as the sum of the utilities associated with each individual consumption good, while expected total utility E (a measure of the overall satisfaction felt by the consumer) can be expressed as the sum of expected utility from goods (E_1) and utility from leisure (E_2). In other words: [1]

$$E_1 = AU_1(q_1^C) + AU_2(q_2^C) + \cdots\cdots + AU_n(q_n^C) \qquad (3.1)$$
$$E = E_1(T_L) + E_2(T_R) \qquad (3.2)$$

Assumptions Relating to Production

Our analysis assumes a Cobb-Douglas production function of form $q_i = b_i T_{Li}^{1-\alpha}$ (the subscript i denotes the good number or type), where the production elements are the capital stock and labor time. For $\alpha > 0$ (i.e. $1-\alpha < 1$) this production function satisfies the principle of diminishing marginal productivity. [2]

The shape of this production function depends on the specific value of α. The short-term equilibrium analysis in this chapter assumes that $\alpha=1/2$, such that the production function takes the form $q_i = b_i T_{Li}^{1/2}$.

Crusoe's Behavioral Principles

Crusoe's behavior as a consumer and a producer is governed by the following principles.

1. For a given "allocation to labor" (out of the total output of goods supplied by Crusoe as producer) and a given proportion of this allocation that is apportioned to consumption ("the average propensity to consume", denoted by a), Crusoe as consumer allocates his time (T) across time spent working (T_L) and time spent resting (T_R) so as to maximize his total expected utility (the sum of utility from goods and utility of leisure). Time equivalent to the amount required

to produce the remaining proportion $(1-a)$ of the "allocation to labor" is "entrusted" to Crusoe as producer.

2. Crusoe as producer uses the labor time (T_L) supplied by Crusoe as consumer to produce goods (total output) that are distributed to Crusoe as consumer in accordance with the "allocation to labor". The time entrusted by Crusoe as consumer to Crusoe as producer is used to produce pure investment goods.

3. Crusoe as producer uses *all* of the time entrusted by Crusoe as consumer to produce pure investment goods.

1. Derivation of the Expected Goods Utility Function and Determination of Output Quantities

In Chapter 1 we used fish—the only food available to Crusoe—as the sole example of a consumption good for which Crusoe experiences a positive rate of utility attrition. In this section we add "fruit" to our model as another consumption good for which Crusoe experiences a positive rate of utility attrition, and use this two-good model (where Good 1 = fish and Good 2 = fruit) to analyze Crusoe's production behavior as well as the optimal consumption equilibrium. We then extend this analysis to derive the expected goods utility function $E_1(T_L)$ for the case of multiple goods.

1.1. Maximizing Expected Goods Utility with Multiple Goods

We now use Equation 2.5 (see Chapter 2, Section 2) to show the goods utility function for each consumption good (fish and fruit):

$$\left.\begin{array}{ll} \text{Fish} \quad \text{(Good 1)} \quad AU_1 = \alpha_1 - \dfrac{1}{2}\dfrac{\beta_1 T}{q_1^{c\prime}} \\[3mm] \text{Fruit} \quad \text{(Good 2)} \quad AU_2 = \alpha_2 - \dfrac{1}{2}\dfrac{\beta_2 T}{q_2^{c\prime}} \end{array}\right\} \qquad (3.3)$$

α_1 and α_2 denote the initial level of utility derived from consumption of one unit of Good 1 and Good 2 (respectively), β_1 and β_2 denote the (constant) utility attrition rates for each good (based on their respective utility attrition functions), and $q_1^{c\prime}$ and $q_2^{c\prime}$ denote the amounts consumed of each good during T units of time.

$q_1^{c\prime}$ and $q_2^{c\prime}$ correspond to the amounts obtained by multiplying the "allocation to labor" of each good—q_1^{c} and q_2^{c}—by the marginal propensity to consume (a). As such, we may write $q_1^{c\prime} = a\, q_1^{c}$ and $q_2^{c\prime} =$

$a\ q_2{}^c$. Under Assumption (5), *all* output is allocated to labor, such that $q_1{}^c$ and $q_2{}^c$ are equal to q_1 and q_2 (the total output of each good). Substituting into the previous equations yields $q_1{}^c{}' = a\ q_1$ and $q_2{}^c{}' = a\ q_2$.

We may then use Crusoe's (non-linear) production function for each good $q_i = b_i T_{Li}^{1/2}$ ($i=1,2$) to obtain $q_i^c = ab_i T_{Li}^{1/2}$. Substituting into Equation 3.3 yields the following goods utility functions:

$$
\left.
\begin{array}{ll}
\text{Fish (Good 1)} & AU_1 = \alpha_1 - \dfrac{1}{2}\dfrac{\beta_1 T}{ab_1 T_{L1}^{1/2}} \\[3mm]
\text{Fruit (Good 2)} & AU_2 = \alpha_2 - \dfrac{1}{2}\dfrac{\beta_2 T}{ab_2 T_{L2}^{1/2}}
\end{array}
\right\}
\tag{3.4}
$$

Under Assumption (1), we may then derive Crusoe's expected level of utility from goods (E_1) by substituting Equation 3.4 into Equation 3.1:

$$
E_1 = (\alpha_1 + \alpha_2) - \frac{1}{2a}\left(\frac{\beta_1}{b_1 T_{L1}^{1/2}} + \frac{\beta_2}{b_2 T_{L2}^{1/2}} \right) T
\tag{3.5}
$$

Crusoe divides his work time (T_L) across the two consumption goods such that:

$$
T_L = T_{L1} + T_{L2}
\tag{3.6}
$$

If we assume that work time (T_L) is constant, then Crusoe—as a rational consumer/producer—will determine his allocation of time to production of each good so as to maximize his expected utility from goods (E_1) subject to the constraint given by Equation 3.6.

The first-order condition for this constrained maximization problem is given by:

$$
\frac{T}{4a}\frac{\beta_1}{b_1 T_{L1}^{3/2}} = \frac{T}{4a}\frac{\beta_2}{b_2 T_{L2}^{3/2}}
\tag{3.7}
$$

The left-hand side of Equation 3.7 represents the change in expected utility from goods that results from a marginal increase in time spent working on production of Good 1 (fish), i.e. $\partial E_1 / \partial T_{L1}$, while the right-hand side represents the change in expected utility from goods that results from a marginal increase in time spent working on production of Good 2 (fruit), i.e. $\partial E_2 / \partial T_{L2}$. In other words, the first-order condition for this maximization problem states that these two marginal utilities must be equal.

Eliminating $T/4a$ from each side of Equation 3.7 and rearranging yields the following:

$$\frac{T_{L2}}{T_{L1}} = \left(\frac{\beta_2}{\beta_1}\right)^{2/3}\left(\frac{b_1}{b_2}\right)^{2/3} \tag{3.8}$$

This shows that the optimal ratio (of time spent working on production of Good 2 to time spent working on production of Good 1) increases with an increase in the ratio of the utility attrition rates (Good 2 to Good 1) and decreases with an increase in the productivity ratio (Good 2 to Good 1).

1.2. Derivation of the Expected Goods Utility Function

Having shown the first-order condition for an expected utility maximization problem with multiple goods, let us assume that Crusoe acts in a rational manner such that this first-order condition is satisfied at all times. In other words, Crusoe attains the maximum level of expected utility from goods (E_1) that is possible for a given amount of labor time (T_L). We refer to $E_1(T_L)$—which describes the relationship between time spent working (T_L) and the maximum possible level of expected utility from goods—as the "expected goods utility function with multiple goods" or simply the "expected goods utility function". This function encapsulates the utility experienced by Crusoe as a result of allocating T_L of his T units of time to work and consuming multiple consumption goods.

In order to find a specific form for $E_1(T_L)$, we begin by expressing the time spent working on production of each good as a function of total work time (T_L), which we take as given. Equation 3.6 (the budget constraint) and Equation 3.8 (the first-order condition) form a pair of simultaneous conditions in T_{L1} and T_{L2}, which can be solved to yield the following:

$$\left.\begin{array}{l} T_{L1} = \dfrac{(\beta_1/b_1)^{2/3}}{(\beta_1/b_1)^{2/3}+(\beta_2/b_2)^{2/3}}T_L \\[4mm] T_{L2} = \dfrac{(\beta_2/b_2)^{2/3}}{(\beta_1/b_1)^{2/3}+(\beta_2/b_2)^{2/3}}T_L \end{array}\right\} \tag{3.9}$$

$E_1(T_L)$—the relationship between time spent working (T_L) and the maximum possible level of expected utility from goods—can then be expressed as the following by substituting Equation 3.9 into Equation 3.5 and rearranging:

$$E_1(T_L) = (\alpha_1 + \alpha_2) - \frac{1}{2a}\left\{(\beta_1/b_1)^{2/3} + (\beta_2/b_2)^{2/3}\right\}^{3/2} \frac{T}{T_L^{1/2}} \quad (3.10)$$

If we set A equal to $\left\{(\beta_1/b_1)^{2/3} + (\beta_2/b_2)^{2/3}\right\}^{3/2}$, then Equation 3.10 can be expressed more simply as:

$$E_1(T_L) = (\alpha_1 + \alpha_2) - \frac{A}{2a}\frac{T}{T_L^{1/2}} \quad (3.11)$$

The shape of the expected goods utility function $E_1(T_L)$ is as shown in Figure 3.1.

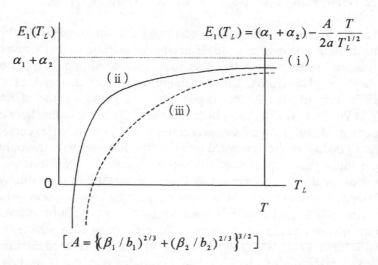

$$\left[A = \left\{(\beta_1/b_1)^{2/3} + (\beta_2/b_2)^{2/3}\right\}^{3/2}\right]$$

Figure 3.1 Expected goods utility function $E_1(T_L)$

If all goods have utility attrition rates equal to zero, or all goods have infinite labor productivities, then A is equal to zero, and the expected goods utility function is a horizontal flat line (i). If $A>0$, then the expected goods utility function is a hyperbola that is convex with respect to $(E_1, T_L) = (\alpha_1+\alpha_2, 0)$. A increases as the utility attrition rate for any good increases or the labor productivity for any good decreases (with all else remaining unchanged), such that the expected goods utility function shifts downward and to the right ((ii)→(iii)). Conversely, A decreases as the utility attrition rate for any good decreases or the labor productivity for any good increases, such that the expected goods utility function shifts upward and to the left ((iii)→(ii)).

1.3. Determination of Output Quantities for Given Labor Time

We next consider how output quantities for each good are determined (for the case where labor time is an exogenous variable) with a view to clarifying the mechanism by which resources are allocated in a non-monetary economy.

Using the production functions for each good $q_i = b_i T_{Li}^{1/2}$ ($i=1,2$), we can express the budget constraint ($T_L = T_{L1}+T_{L2}$) in terms of the quantity of each good:

$$
\left.
\begin{aligned}
T_L &= \left(\frac{q_1}{b_1}\right)^2 + \left(\frac{q_2}{b_2}\right)^2 \\[2ex]
\text{or} \quad q_2 &= \left\{ b_2^2 T_L - \left(\frac{b_2}{b_1}\right)^2 q_1^2 \right\}^{1/2}
\end{aligned}
\right\}
\tag{3.12}
$$

We can also express the first-order condition (Equation 3.8) in terms of the quantity of each good by using the ratio of the two production functions $q_i = b_i T_{Li}^{1/2}$ ($i=1,2$):

$$
\left.
\begin{aligned}
\frac{q_2}{q_1} &= \left(\frac{\beta_2}{\beta_1}\right)^{1/3}\left(\frac{b_2}{b_1}\right)^{2/3} \\[2ex]
\text{or} \quad q_2 &= \left(\frac{\beta_2}{\beta_1}\right)^{1/3}\left(\frac{b_2}{b_1}\right)^{2/3} q_1
\end{aligned}
\right\}
\tag{3.13}
$$

Solving Equations 3.12 and 3.13 for a given level of labor time (T_L) yields the following:

$$
\left.
\begin{aligned}
q_1 &= \left\{ \frac{(\beta_1/b_1)^{2/3}}{(\beta_1/b_1)^{2/3}+(\beta_2/b_2)^{2/3}} \right\}^{1/2} b_1 T_L^{1/2} \\[2ex]
q_2 &= \left\{ \frac{(\beta_2/b_2)^{2/3}}{(\beta_1/b_1)^{2/3}+(\beta_2/b_2)^{2/3}} \right\}^{1/2} b_2 T_L^{1/2}
\end{aligned}
\right\}
\tag{3.14}
$$

These output quantities for each good are the same as those determined by substituting the optimal levels of T_{L1} and T_{L2} (time spent working on production of each good, as shown in Equation 3.9) into the production functions.

Under Assumption (5), the entire output of each good (as shown in Equation 3.14) is allocated to Crusoe (as consumer) in the form of "allocation to labor".

2. Derivation of the Leisure Utility Function

Having derived the goods utility function $E_1(T_L)$, we now define the leisure utility function as $E_2(T_R)$ and consider Crusoe's expected total utility $(E_1(T_L) + E_2(T_R))$. In order to define $E_2(T_R)$, we must make the following three assumptions (which should not appear unreasonable).

1. Crusoe's utility from leisure is an increasing function of the time that he spends resting, i.e. ($\partial E_2 / \partial T_R > 0$).
2. The marginal utility of leisure (the increase in $E_2(T_R)$ that results from an extremely small increase in time spent resting) decreases as T_R increases, but never falls to zero, i.e. ($\partial^2 E_2 / \partial T_R^2 < 0$, $\lim_{T_R \to +\infty} \partial E_2 / \partial T_R = 0$). These assumptions relate to the principle of diminishing marginal utility and non-saturation.
3. In order to survive, Crusoe must spend more than l (= required level of leisure time) units of time resting, and his marginal utility of leisure approaches infinity as his time spent resting approaches this level (from above). Generally speaking, the required level of leisure time may be attributed to physiological needs such as sleep, excretion, and other activities that are essential to survival. ($T_R > l$, $\lim_{T_R \to l} \partial E_2 / \partial T_R = +\infty$)

There are many possible leisure utility functions that satisfy these assumptions, but here we assume that the leisure utility function takes a similar form to the expected goods utility function $E_1(T_L)$ with a view to expressing the equilibrium levels of work time and output in a relatively simple form.

$$E_2(T_R) = \gamma - \frac{\varepsilon}{2} \frac{T}{(T_R - l)^{1/2}} \tag{3.15}$$

Note that $T_R > l$. Here, ε is a positive parameter that determines the shape of the function, while γ is a positive parameter that represents an upper bound for the level of utility as $T_R \to +\infty$.

We assume that these parameters and Crusoe's required level of leisure time (l) are extremely stable—although they may vary due to Crusoe's physical health or other circumstances—and that they are not affected by the amount of time spent working or other circumstances relating to work.

As shown in Figure 3.2 (which shows the origin on the right-hand side), Crusoe's leisure utility function is a hyperbola that is convex with respect to $(E_2, T_R) = (\gamma, l)$.

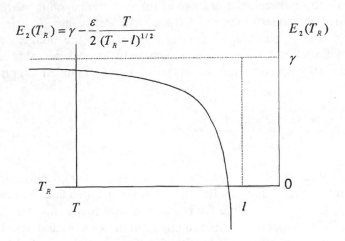

$$E_2(T_R) = \gamma - \frac{\varepsilon}{2} \frac{T}{(T_R - l)^{1/2}}$$

Figure 3.2 Leisure utility function $E_2(T_R)$

3. Maximization of Expected Total Utility and Simultaneous Determination of Output Quantities and Resource Allocation

3.1. Definition of Expected Total Utility Function and Maximization Conditions

Under Assumption (2), Crusoe's expected total utility E is equal to the sum of expected utility from goods $E_1(T_L)$ and utility of leisure $E_2(T_R)$. As such, we obtain Crusoe's expected total utility function by substituting Equations 3.11 and 3.15 into Equation 3.2:

$$E = (\alpha_1 + \alpha_2 + \gamma) - \frac{A}{2a} \frac{T}{T_L^{1/2}} - \frac{\varepsilon}{2} \frac{T}{(T_R - l)^{1/2}} \tag{3.16}$$

where $A = \left\{ (\beta_1 / b_1)^{2/3} + (\beta_2 / b_2)^{2/3} \right\}^{3/2}$ and $T_R > l$.

Crusoe's T units of time are allocated across time spent working T_L and time spent resting T_R, such that:

$$T = T_L + T_R \tag{3.17}$$

T, which represents the passage of time, is an exogenous variable. As a rational consumer/producer, Crusoe will determine T_L (time spent working) and T_R (time spent resting)—subject to the budget constraint given by Equation 3.17—so as to maximize his expected total utility (E).

The first-order condition for this constrained maximization problem is given by:

$$\frac{A}{4a} \frac{T}{T_L^{3/2}} = \frac{\varepsilon}{4} \frac{T}{(T_R - l)^{3/2}} \tag{3.18}$$

The left-hand side of Equation 3.18 represents the change in expected utility from goods that results from a marginal increase in time spent working, i.e. $\partial E_1 / \partial T_L$, while the right-hand side represents the change in utility of leisure that results from a marginal increase in time spent resting, i.e. $\partial E_2 / \partial T_R$. In other words, the first-order condition for this maximization problem states that these two marginal utilities must be equal.

3.2. The "Basic Equation of Labor" and Robinson Crusoe's Subjective Equilibrium

Let us assume that Crusoe acts in a rational manner such that this first-order condition is satisfied at all times. The equilibrium levels of T_L (time spent working) and T_R (time spent resting) that maximize Crusoe's expected total utility are determined by solving Equations 3.17 and 3.18 as a pair of simultaneous equations, and can be expressed as follows if we set A equal to $\left\{ (\beta_1 / b_1)^{2/3} + (\beta_2 / b_2)^{2/3} \right\}^{3/2}$:

$$T_L^* = \frac{(\beta_1 / b_1)^{2/3} + (\beta_2 / b_2)^{2/3}}{(\beta_1 / b_1)^{2/3} + (\beta_2 / b_2)^{2/3} + (a\varepsilon)^{2/3}} (T - l) \tag{3.19}$$

$$T_R^* = \frac{(a\varepsilon)^{2/3}}{(\beta_1 / b_1)^{2/3} + (\beta_2 / b_2)^{2/3} + (a\varepsilon)^{2/3}} (T - l) + l \tag{3.20}$$

Equation 3.19 shows that the equilibrium level of time spent working (T_L^*) is directly proportional to the utility attrition rate for any good and inversely proportional to labor productivity. Where both goods have a zero utility attrition rate, the right-hand side of Equation 3.19 has a zero numerator, such that the equilibrium level of time spent working (T_L^*) is also equal to zero, which means that Crusoe does not spend any time working.

In this book we refer to Equation 3.19 as the "basic equation of labor", as it describes the relationship between the amount of labor supplied by Crusoe and the (positive) rates of utility attrition (the fundamental drivers of demand within our framework).

Figure 3.3 shows Crusoe's subjective equilibrium based on this "basic equation of labor". Crusoe's expected total utility E is drawn as the sum of his expected utility from goods $E_1(T_L)$ and his utility from leisure $E_2(T_R)$. T_L^* denotes the equilibrium level of time spent working, that is, the level at which Crusoe maximizes his expected total utility.

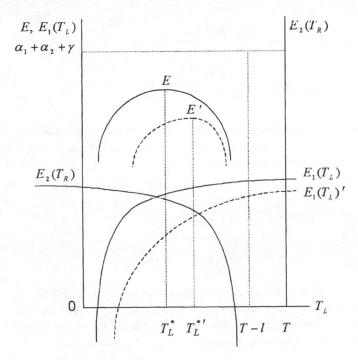

Figure 3.3 Crusoe's subjective equilibrium based on the "basic equation of labor"

An increase in one (or both) of the utility attrition rates would cause the expected goods utility function to shift from $E_1(T_L)$ to $E_1(T_L)'$ (as shown by the dotted line), such that the expected total utility function would shift from E to E'. As a result, the amount of time that Crusoe would have to spend working in order to maximize his expected total utility would increase from T_L^* to $T_L^{*\prime}$. It should therefore be clear that the (positive) rates of utility attrition uniquely determine the amount of labor supplied by Crusoe via his subjective equilibrium.

3.3. Framework for Simultaneous Determination of Output Quantities and Resource Allocation

In Section 1.3 we derived equations showing the output quantities for each good for a given amount of labor time (Equation 3.14). The "basic equation of labor" (Equation 3.19) shows the equilibrium level of labor time supplied by Crusoe, and substituting this into Equation 3.14 therefore gives the equilibrium output quantities for each good:

$$
\left.
\begin{aligned}
q_1^* &= \left\{ \frac{(\beta_1/b_1)^{2/3}}{(\beta_1/b_1)^{2/3}+(\beta_2/b_2)^{2/3}+(a\varepsilon)^{2/3}} \right\}^{1/2} b_1(T-l)^{1/2} \\
q_2^* &= \left\{ \frac{(\beta_2/b_2)^{2/3}}{(\beta_1/b_1)^{2/3}+(\beta_2/b_2)^{2/3}+(a\varepsilon)^{2/3}} \right\}^{1/2} b_2(T-l)^{1/2}
\end{aligned}
\right\} \quad (3.21)
$$

Given the non-linear production functions for each good $q_i = b_i T_{Li}^{1/2}$, we can express the equilibrium levels of time spent working on production of each good as follows:

$$
\left.
\begin{aligned}
T_{L1}^* &= \frac{(\beta_1/b_1)^{2/3}}{(\beta_1/b_1)^{2/3}+(\beta_2/b_2)^{2/3}+(a\varepsilon)^{2/3}}(T-l) \\
T_{L2}^* &= \frac{(\beta_2/b_2)^{2/3}}{(\beta_1/b_1)^{2/3}+(\beta_2/b_2)^{2/3}+(a\varepsilon)^{2/3}}(T-l)
\end{aligned}
\right\} \quad (3.22)
$$

These equilibrium levels determine the total level of time that Crusoe spends working (the supply of labor), and also indicate the optimal allocation of production factors and the quantities of each consumption good that are produced as a result.

3.4. Meaning and Impact of Changes in the Ratio Between Utility Parameters

In considering the impact of changes in the utility attrition rates β_1 and β_2 on the equilibrium levels of labor (employment) and output, it is useful to designate one consumption good as a "reference good" and consider the ratio of utility attrition rates. Changes in utility attrition rates can then be broken down into: (1) changes in the reference good's utility attrition rate; and (2) changes in the ratio of another good's utility attrition rate to that of the reference good.

If we designate Good 1 as the reference good, then the ratio of Good 2's utility attrition rate to that of the reference good is given by β_2/β_1, and Good 2's utility attrition rate (β_2) is given by the product of this ratio and the reference good's attrition rate. If β_1 and β_2 increase in the same proportion, then β_1 increases while β_2/β_1 remains unchanged. For the purpose of our analysis, we now take the "basic equation of labor" (Equation 3.19) and divide both the numerator and the denominator on the right-hand side through by β_1 (the reference good's utility attrition rate), yielding:

$$T_L^* = \frac{(1/b_1)^{2/3} + (\beta_2/\beta_1)^{2/3}(1/b_2)^{2/3}}{(1/b_1)^{2/3} + (\beta_2/\beta_1)^{2/3}(1/b_2)^{2/3} + \{a(\varepsilon/\beta_1)\}^{2/3}}(T-l) \qquad (3.23)$$

Equation 3.23 can be generalized to give a generalized "basic equation of labor" for the case of m different goods:

$$T_L^* = \frac{\displaystyle\sum_{j=1}^{m}(\beta_j/\beta_i)^{2/3}(1/b_j)^{2/3}}{\displaystyle\sum_{j=1}^{m}(\beta_j/\beta_i)^{2/3}(1/b_j)^{2/3} + \{a(\varepsilon/\beta_i)\}^{2/3}}(T-l) \qquad (3.24)$$

Here the subscript j denotes the jth of the m goods, and i denotes the number of the reference good.

According to Equation 3.24, the (generalized) equilibrium level of labor time supplied by Crusoe (T_L^*) is determined by the ratios of utility attrition rates to that of the reference good (β_j/β_i) and the ratio of the reference good's utility attrition rate to the leisure utility function parameter β_i/ε, which we term the "relative utility attrition rate". In Section 2 we make the assumption that ε is extremely stable and is not affected by the amount of time spent working or other circumstances relating to work. As such, an increase in β_i (the reference good's utility attrition rate) can be expected to reduce ε/β_i (the reciprocal of the relative utility attrition rate), thereby increasing the equilibrium level of labor time (T_L^*). Alternatively, if β_i remains constant while other utility attrition rates increase, then the resulting increases in the ratios β_j/β_i serve to increase the equilibrium level of labor time (T_L^*).

By decomposing changes in utility attrition rates into (1) changes in the reference good's utility attrition rate and (2) changes in the ratio of another good's utility attrition rate to that of the reference good, and considering these changes within the generalized "basic equation of labor" (Equation 3.24), it is therefore possible to analyze how a change in the utility attrition rate for any given good affects the equilibrium level of labor time (T_L^*).

It should also be noted that the generalized "basic equation of labor" (Equation 3.24) only requires us to specify the *ratios* β_j / β_i and β_i / ε, and does not require us to specify the absolute *levels* of utility attrition rates (β_i, β_j) or the leisure utility function parameter (ε). As we shall discuss in the following chapter, these ratios $(\beta_j / \beta_i$ and $\beta_i / \varepsilon)$ can be measured using observable data on output levels, labor time (employment), and labor productivity. This enables us to overcome the fact that utility itself cannot be measured and conduct empirical analysis of the psychological elements that govern human (economic) behavior and the causal connections between them.[3]

4. Determination of Pure Investment Good Output Quantity and the Supply-Demand Adjustment Process

With no need to set aside a stock of consumption goods for future use, Crusoe as consumer can "invest" some of his time in Crusoe as producer, who uses this time to produce pure investment goods. In this section we look at the output level of a pure investment good and consider the supply-demand adjustment process.

4.1. Commissioned Labor and Determination of Pure Investment Good Output Quantity

Under Assumption (5), all output of each good (Equation 3.21) is distributed to Crusoe as consumer in the form of an "allocation to labor". As such, Crusoe as consumer can "invest" some of his time—specifically, the time required to produce consumption goods for future consumption—in Crusoe as producer. This may be viewed as a commission of labor.

The amounts of Good 1 and Good 2 that are not consumed during the current period (T units of time) are given by $(1-a) \, q_1^*$ and $(1-a) \, q_2^*$. If we denote the times required to produce these quantities by T_{L1}^S and T_{L2}^S, and note that the production functions for Good 1 and Good 2 have average productivities of (q_1^* / T_{L1}^*) and (q_2^* / T_{L2}^*), then we may write $(1-a)$ $q_1^* = (q_1^* / T_{L1}^*) T_{L1}^S$ and $(1-a) \, q_2^* = (q_2^* / T_{L2}^*) T_{L2}^S$, which means that the times required to produce quantities of Good 1 and Good 2 for future consumption are given by $T_{L1}^S = (1-a) \, T_{L1}^*$ and $T_{L2}^S = (1-a) \, T_{L2}^*$.[4] If the time that Crusoe as consumer invests in Crusoe as producer ("commissioned labor time") is denoted by $T_L^S = T_{L1}^S + T_{L2}^S$, then we may write:

$$T_L^S = (1-a)T_L^* \qquad (3.25)$$

We now introduce a pure investment good (Good 3) with output (demand) denoted by q_3^{IP} and its production function defined by $q_3^{IP} = b_3(T_L^S)^{1/2}$. Substituting Equation 3.25 into the production function yields the following:

$$q_3^{IP} = b_3(1-a)^{1/2}(T_L^*)^{1/2}$$

$$= b_3(1-a)^{1/2}\left\{\frac{(\beta_1/b_1)^{2/3} + (\beta_2/b_2)^{2/3}}{(\beta_1/b_1)^{2/3} + (\beta_2/b_2)^{2/3} + (a\varepsilon)^{2/3}}\right\}^{1/2}(T-l)^{1/2} \quad (3.26)$$

In accordance with the behavioral principles stated in Section 1 of this chapter, Crusoe as producer uses *all* of the time entrusted (invested) by Crusoe as consumer (as given by Equation 3.25) to produce pure investment goods, with total output given by Equation 3.26. As such, output of the pure investment good (q_3^{IP}) is determined by the equilibrium level of labor time (T_L^*, which is in turn determined through optimal behavior on the part of Crusoe), productivity for the pure investment good (b_3), and Crusoe's average propensity to consume.

4.2. The Supply-Demand Adjustment Process for Pure Investment Goods

The above analysis is based on the assumption that Crusoe as producer uses (demands) *all* of the time entrusted (invested) by Crusoe as consumer to produce pure investment goods. However, the level of pure investment is determined (decided) by Crusoe as producer, and it is possible to imagine circumstances under which his demand for labor time (to produce quantity q_3^{IP} of pure investment goods) might not match the supply of labor time by Crusoe as consumer (the amount of commissioned labor time).

We now assume that Crusoe's utility attrition rates (β_1 and β_2), productivities (b_1, b_2, and b_3), and leisure utility function parameter (ε) remain constant, and consider the adjustment process for a situation where demand for labor (from Crusoe as producer) to produce quantity q_3^{IP} of pure investment goods exceeds the amount of commissioned labor time, that is, where $(q_3^{IP}/b_3)^2 > T_L^S$. It can be seen from Equation 3.26 that the adjustment process will require a fall in the average propensity to consume (a). Conversely, if demand for labor (from Crusoe as producer) to produce quantity q_3^{IP} of pure investment goods is less than the amount of commissioned labor time, that is, if $(q_3^{IP} / b_3)^2 < T_L^S$, then the adjustment process will require a rise in the average propensity to consume (a).

In this example, because the consumer and the producer is the same entity (Robinson Crusoe), it is natural to assume that Crusoe's average propensity to consume (a) will already reflect the desired level of pure investment; in other words, we may assume that the above adjustment process has already been completed. As such, we may assume that the amount of commissioned labor time supplied by Crusoe based on his average propensity to consume (a) is always equal to the time needed in order to produce quantity q_3^{IP} of pure investment goods.

NOTES

1. This assumption means that our analysis does not cover goods that are complements or substitutes (see Chapter 8, Section 3).
2. Given Assumption (5), if we use K_0 to denote the initial capital stock and δ to denote the capital attrition rate, then the average level of the capital stock during the analysis period is given by $\{1 - (\delta / 2)\}K_0$. Substituting this into the Cobb-Douglas production function of form $q = A\,K^{\alpha}\,T_L^{1-\alpha}$ yields $q = A\,\{1 - (\delta / 2)\}^{\alpha}\,K_0^{\alpha}\,T_L^{1-\alpha}$, where $A\,\{1 - (\delta / 2)\}^{\alpha}\,K_0^{\alpha}$ is a constant. As such, the general production function—which takes the capital stock and labor time as arguments—can be expressed as a non-linear production function with labor time as the "essential" production element. In this book we use b to denote $A\,\{1 - (\delta / 2)\}^{\alpha}\,K_0^{\alpha}$. From the definition of this constant, it is clear that a higher initial level of the capital stock (K_0) implies a higher level of b.
3. The measurability of β_j / β_i (the ratio of the utility attrition rate for Good j to that of Good i, the reference good) and β_i / ε (the relative utility attrition rate for Good i) is discussed in Chapter 4, Section 3.
4. Because the production function satisfies the principle of diminishing marginal productivity, the amount of commissioned labor is lower when marginal productivity is high and higher when marginal productivity is low. In order to eliminate the impact of such differences, we have used *average* productivity in our analysis.

Chapter 4

Extension to Analysis of a Monetary Economy

In this chapter we perform an analysis (similar to that in the previous chapter) based on "The Human Income-Expenditure Balance in a Monetary Economy (a Household/Firm Model)" (Figure 1.10 of Chapter 1, Section 2), and show that our "basic equation of labor"—which we derived under the assumption of a non-monetary economy—is also applicable to a monetary economy. We then complete our theoretical framework by incorporating a mechanism—similar to that used in classical macroeconomic theory—for the determination of interest rates and price levels (money wages), before concluding the chapter with a discussion as to the measurability of utility parameters.

Assumptions Behind Our Analysis

For the purposes of this chapter we maintain Assumptions (1) and (2) from Chapter 3 (along with Equations 3.1 and 3.2), which ensure additivity of utility and, with a view to constructing a simple model of transactions between households and firms in an economy populated by a large number of people, we add the following assumptions:

(3) The economy is made up of a large number of households that survive by consuming two consumption goods (Good 1 and Good 2) and a large number of firms that produce two consumption goods (Good 1 and Good 2) and one pure investment good (Good 3).
(4) Each household has a linear utility attrition function (a constant utility attrition rate) for each consumption good.
(5) Each household receives an identical money wage (per unit of work time) irrespective of labor productivity and the type of good that is being produced (changes in labor productivity ratios across production divisions result in changes to goods price ratios, not changes to the money wage).

(6) Each of a firm's production divisions (for Good 1, Good 2, and Good 3) has its own production facilities and operates on a stand-alone (self-sufficient) basis.

(7) Firms already own the raw materials required to produce each good, and do not book any costs in relation to such materials.

(8) A capital stock exists at the start of the analysis period, and the capital attrition rate is zero. In terms of Figure 1.10, this means that the proportion allocated to capital is zero, and there is no flow of "replacement investment". In other words, all output is allocated to households.

(9) Pure investment during the analysis period does not add to the capital stock, and has no impact on utility attrition rates or labor productivity during the analysis period.

(10) Firms aim to maximize their profits, and all of their profits based on the production of consumption goods are distributed to households, while firms save the profits based on the production of pure investment goods.

(11) Firms pay households for the fixed costs associated with production of the two consumption goods (Good 1 and Good 2).

For the sake of convenience, we have assumed that each firm consists of three independent "production divisions". This is meant to capture the idea of three separate industries, each populated by a large number of independent firms.

Assumptions Relating to Production

As in Chapter 3, we conduct short-term equilibrium analysis based on the assumption that production functions take the form $q_i = b_i T_{Li}^{1/2}$, where the subscript i denotes the good number or type.

Behavioral Principles for Households and Firms

Households (consumers) and firms (producers) behave as follows.

1. Each household receives a wage (W) in exchange for the supply of labor time (T_L), and also receives a distribution of corporate profits (P) and a payment of fixed costs ($\overline{C}$). Of this total income (I), an amount dependent on the household's average propensity to consume (a) is allocated to spending on household consumption (C_W). This is then used to purchase the particular combination of goods that maximizes the household's expected utility from goods (for given goods prices and a given utility attrition rate), and the remaining amount is invested as household savings (S_W). The amount of labor

time (T_L) supplied by the household is determined so as to maximize its expected total utility (for a given money wage, given goods prices, and a given utility attrition rate), which is defined as the sum of expected utility from goods and utility from leisure.

2. Firms use the labor time supplied by households (T_L) to produce consumption goods (Good 1 and Good 2) in accordance with their respective production functions, and earn income by selling these goods to households. Firms incur factor costs, which are paid to households as wages (W) and fixed costs $(\overline{C})$. Firms earn profits (P) equal to their total sales revenue minus their factor costs, but all of these profits are distributed to households. Firms raise funds equal to household savings (S_w) by issuing shares or bonds, and use these funds to invest (I_P) in production of the pure investment good (q^{IP}).

3. Firms demand all of the funds saved by households (S_w), and allocate all of these funds to pure investment (I_P).

1. Analysis of a Monetary Economy and Determination of Output Quantities and Resource Allocations

In this section we construct a framework for the determination of output quantities and resource allocations in a monetary economy, and show that our "basic equation of labor"—which we derived in Chapter 3 under the assumption of a non-monetary economy—is also applicable to a monetary economy. A summary of our theoretical framework is presented in Chapter 8.

1.1. Analysis of Household Behavior

Under Assumption (4), the goods utility function derived in Section 2 of Chapter 2 Equation 2.5 can be used to show a household's utility function for each of the two consumption goods:

$$\left. \begin{array}{l} AU_1 = \alpha_1 - \dfrac{1}{2}\dfrac{\beta_1 T}{q_1^{c'}} \\[3mm] AU_2 = \alpha_2 - \dfrac{1}{2}\dfrac{\beta_2 T}{q_2^{c'}} \end{array} \right\} \tag{4.1}$$

In Equation 4.1, α_1 and α_2 denote the initial utility levels that are attained as a result of consumption of one unit of Good 1 and Good 2 (respectively), while β_1 and β_2 are the household's (constant) utility attrition rates for Good 1 and Good 2 (respectively), and $q_1^{c'}$ and $q_2^{c'}$ are the amounts of each good consumed during units of time T.

$q_1^{c'}$ and $q_2^{c'}$ correspond to the amounts obtained by multiplying the "allocation to labor" of each good—q_1^c and q_2^c—by the average propensity to consume (a). As such, we may write $q_1^{c'} = a\, q_1^c$ and $q_2^{c'} = a\, q_2^c$. Under Assumption (8), *all* output is allocated to labor, such that q_1^c and q_2^c are equal to q_1 and q_2 (the total output of each good). Substituting into the previous equations yields $q_1^{c'} = a\, q_1$ and $q_2^{c'} = a\, q_2$, such that we may write the household's goods utility functions for Good 1 and Good 2 as follows:

$$\left. \begin{aligned} AU_1 &= \alpha_1 - \frac{1}{2}\frac{\beta_1 T}{aq_1} \\[2mm] AU_2 &= \alpha_2 - \frac{1}{2}\frac{\beta_2 T}{aq_2} \end{aligned} \right\} \tag{4.2}$$

Under Assumption (1), we may then derive the household's expected level of utility from goods (E_1) by substituting Equation 4.2 into Equation 3.1:

$$E_1 = (\alpha_1 + \alpha_2) - \frac{T}{2a}\left(\frac{\beta_1}{q_1} + \frac{\beta_2}{q_2}\right) \tag{4.3}$$

If a firm sells Good 1 and Good 2 for p_1 and p_2 (respectively), then its total revenue during units of time T is given by $p_1 q_1^{c'} + p_2 q_2^{c'}$. This is equal to the proportion of a household's total income (I) that is allocated to consumption (C_w) in accordance with its average propensity to consume (a), such that we may write $p_1 q_1^{c'} + p_2 q_2^{c'} = aI\ (=C_w)$. We then obtain the following equation by substituting in $q_1^{c'} = a\, q_1$ and $q_2^{c'} = a\, q_2$ and eliminating a:

$$I = p_1 q_1 + p_2 q_2 \tag{4.4}$$

If we assume that the household's total income (I) is constant, then the household—as a rational consumer—will determine its consumption of each good during units of time T so as to maximize its expected utility from goods (E_1) subject to the constraint given by Equation 4.4.

The first-order condition for this constrained maximization problem is given by:[1]

$$\frac{q_2}{q_1} = \left(\frac{\beta_2}{\beta_1}\right)^{1/2}\left(\frac{p_1}{p_2}\right)^{1/2} \tag{4.5}$$

It can be seen from Equation 4.5 that the ratio of optimal output quantities (Good 2 to Good 1) is an increasing function of the ratio of utility attrition rates (Good 2 to Good 1) and a decreasing function of the ratio of prices (Good 2 to Good 1).

The household's demand functions for each good (given total income *I*) can be expressed as follows by solving the budget constraint Equation 4.4 and the first-order condition Equation 4.5 as a pair of simultaneous equations:

$$\left.\begin{aligned}q_1 &= \frac{(p_1\beta_1)^{1/2}}{(p_1\beta_1)^{1/2}+(p_2\beta_2)^{1/2}}\frac{I}{p_1} \\[2mm] q_2 &= \frac{(p_2\beta_2)^{1/2}}{(p_1\beta_1)^{1/2}+(p_2\beta_2)^{1/2}}\frac{I}{p_2}\end{aligned}\right\} \tag{4.6}$$

It can be seen from Equation 4.6 that a household's demand for each consumption good satisfies the law of demand, in that demand for a given good decreases as its price rises, and increases as its price falls.

The expected goods utility function $E_1(I)$—which gives the household's (maximized) utility from goods as a function of its total income (*I*)—is derived by substituting Equation 4.6 into Equation 4.3 and rearranging:

$$\begin{aligned}E_1(I) &= (\alpha_1+\alpha_2)-\frac{T}{2a}\left\{(p_1\beta_1)^{1/2}+(p_2\beta_2)^{1/2}\right\}^2\frac{1}{I} \\[2mm] &= (\alpha_1+\alpha_2)-\frac{A}{2a}\frac{T}{I}\end{aligned} \tag{4.7}$$

where $A = \left\{(p_1\beta_1)^{1/2}+(p_2\beta_2)^{1/2}\right\}^2$

As in the previous chapter, the leisure utility function $E_2(T_R)$ is assumed to take the following form:

$$E_2(T_R) = \gamma - \frac{\varepsilon}{2}\frac{T}{(T_R-l)^{1/2}} \tag{4.8}$$

Note that $T_R > l$. Here ε is a positive parameter that determines the shape of the function, while γ is a positive parameter that represents an upper bound for the level of utility as $T_R \to +\infty$.

Under Assumption (2), the household's expected total utility E is equal to the sum of expected utility from goods $E_1(I)$ and utility of leisure $E_2(T_R)$. As such, we obtain the household's expected total utility function by substituting Equations 4.7 and 4.8 into Equation 3.2:

$$E = (\alpha_1 + \alpha_2 + \gamma) - \frac{A}{2a}\frac{T}{I} - \frac{\varepsilon}{2}\frac{T}{(T_R - I)^{1/2}} \tag{4.9}$$

where $A = \left\{(p_1\beta_1)^{1/2} + (p_2\beta_2)^{1/2}\right\}^2$ and $T_R > I$

Under Assumption (5), all households receive an identical money wage (w). As such, a household supplying work time T_L receives wage income of $W = wT_L$. Total household income is defined as $I = (P + \overline{C}) + W$, which yields the following expression (using the fact that $T_L = T - T_R$):

$$I = (P + \overline{C}) + wT - wT_R \tag{4.10}$$

T, which represents the passage of time, is an exogenous variable. As a rational consumer, a household will determine T_R (time spent resting) and I (total household income, which depends on time spent working)— subject to the budget constraint given by Equation 4.10—so as to maximize its expected total utility (E).

The first-order condition for this constrained maximization problem is given by:

$$\frac{A}{2a}\frac{T}{I^2} = \frac{\varepsilon}{4w}\frac{T}{(T_R - I)^{3/2}} \tag{4.11}$$

The left-hand side of Equation 4.11 represents the change in expected utility from goods that results from a marginal increase in total household income, i.e. $\partial E_1 / \partial I$, while the right-hand side represents the change in utility of leisure that results from a marginal increase in time spent resting, i.e. $\partial E_2 / \partial T_R$. In other words, the first-order condition for this maximization problem states that these two marginal utilities must be equal.

The relationship between time spent working (T_L) and the level of total household income that maximizes a household's expected total utility is obtained by substituting $T_R = T - T_L$ into Equation 4.11 and rearranging:

$$T_L = (T - l) - \left(\frac{a\varepsilon}{2wA}\right)^{2/3} I^{4/3} \tag{4.12}$$

where $A = \left\{(p_1\beta_1)^{1/2} + (p_2\beta_2)^{1/2}\right\}^2$

1.2. Analysis of Corporate Behavior

We next derive a firm's labor demand function based on the assumption of profit maximization. A firm has a separate production division for each of the two consumption goods (Good 1 and Good 2), with each production division demanding labor from households so as to maximize its profits (defined as revenues minus costs). In other words, the following relationship applies, where R_i denotes a firm's revenues from sales of Good i (i=1,2), W_i denotes wages paid to households engaged in production of Good i, $\overline{C_i}$ denotes fixed costs paid to households engaged in production of Good i, and P_i denotes corporate profits derived from production of Good i:

$$P_i = R_i - W_i - \overline{C_i} \tag{4.13}$$

If quantity q_i of Good i is sold at price p_i, then $R_i = p_i q_i$. Furthermore, if we denote each production division's demand for labor by T_{Li} and assume (in accordance with Assumption (5)) that each sector pays an identical money wage w, then $W_i = wT_{Li}$. The production function $q_i = b_i T_{Li}^{1/2}$ implies that $T_{Li} = (q_i/b_i)^2$, which gives $W_i = w(q_i/b_i)^2$. Substituting these expressions for R_i and W_i into Equation 4.13 yields the following profit function for each of a firm's production divisions:

$$P_i = p_i q_i - w(q_i / b_i)^2 - \overline{C_i} \tag{4.14}$$

A profit-maximizing firm demands the amount of labor T_{Li} that maximizes profits P_i. This means that an expression for the production (output) quantity that maximizes profits can be derived by calculating the derivative of the profit function with respect to q_i, setting this derivative equal to zero, and rearranging:

$$q_i = \frac{p_i b_i^2}{2w} \tag{4.15}$$

The amount of labor demanded by a profit-maximizing production division is found by substituting the production function $q_i = b_i T_{Li}^{1/2}$ into Equation 4.15 and rearranging:

$$T_{Li} = \frac{(p_i b_i)^2}{4w^2} \tag{4.16}$$

The amount of labor demanded by an entire firm is obviously the sum of the amount of labor demanded by each of its production divisions, such that $T_L = T_{L1} + T_{L2}$. Substituting Equation 4.16 ($i=1,2$) into this expression and rearranging gives Equation 4.17, which describes the relationship between the real wage w/p_1 (measured in terms of the price of Good 1) and the amount of labor demanded by the entire firm (T_L):

$$w/p_1 = \frac{\left\{ b_1^2 + (p_2/p_1)^2 b_2^2 \right\}^{1/2}}{2T_L^{1/2}} \tag{4.17}$$

Figure 4.1 shows the firm's labor demand function under the assumption that the price ratio p_2/p_1 remains constant.

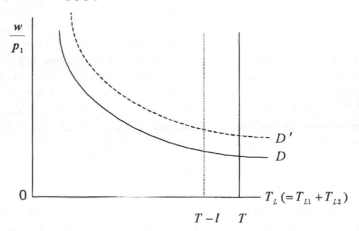

Figure 4.1 Firm's labor demand function

Equation 4.17 implies that an increase in the labor productivity parameter for either good (b_i, $i=1,2$) causes the firm's labor supply curve to shift upwards from (solid line) D to (dotted line) D' in Figure 4.1.

1.3. Derivation of the Equilibrium Price Ratio

We next calculate the "equilibrium price ratio", that is, the price ratio that equates aggregate demand (based on the subjective equilibria of households) with aggregate supply (based on the subjective equilibria of firms) for each good.

The ratio q_2/q_1—the quantity of Good 2 demanded by a household divided by the quantity of Good 1 demanded by that household (based on the household's subjective equilibrium)—is determined by the first-order condition shown in Equation 4.5:

$$\frac{q_2}{q_1} = \left(\frac{\beta_2}{\beta_1}\right)^{1/2}\left(\frac{p_1}{p_2}\right)^{1/2} \tag{4.5}$$

Figure 4.2 shows the "goods preference curve"—the combinations of amounts of each good that may be demanded by a household—based on Equation 4.5.

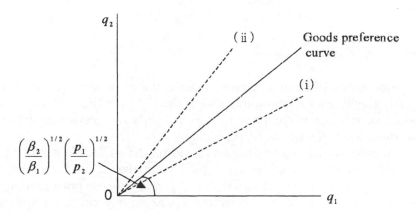

Figure 4.2 Goods preference curve

Equation 4.5 implies that an increase in the price ratio p_2/p_1 shifts the goods preference curve downwards and to the right (to (i) in Figure 4.2), while a decrease in the price ratio p_2/p_1 shifts the goods preference curve upwards and to the left (to (ii) in Figure 4.2).

We next use Equation 4.15 to calculate q_2/q_1, the quantity of Good 2 supplied by a firm divided by the quantity of Good 1 supplied by that firm (based on the firm's subjective equilibrium):

$$\frac{q_2}{q_1} = \left(\frac{b_2}{b_1}\right)^2 \left(\frac{p_2}{p_1}\right) \tag{4.18}$$

Figure 4.3 shows the "goods supply curve"—the combinations of amounts of each good that may be supplied by a firm—based on Equation 4.18.

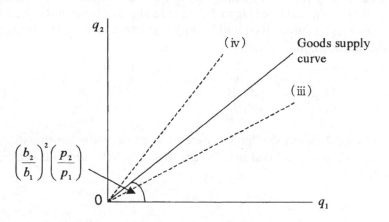

Figure 4.3 Goods supply curve

Equation 4.18 implies that a decrease in the price ratio p_2/p_1 shifts the goods supply curve downwards and to the right (to (iii) in Figure 4.3), while an increase in the price ratio p_2/p_1 shifts the goods supply curve upwards and to the left (to (iv) in Figure 4.3).

In order for aggregate demand (based on the subjective equilibria of households) to be equal to aggregate supply (based on the subjective equilibria of firms) for each good, it is necessary for the price ratio p_2/p_1 to be such that the goods preference curve exactly coincides with the goods supply curve. This is possible since the two curves react in opposite fashion to changes in the price ratio p_2/p_1. The equilibrium price ratio $(p_2/p_1)^*$ that equates aggregate demand with aggregate supply can be found by eliminating q_2/q_1 from Equations 4.5 and 4.18:

$$\left(\frac{p_2}{p_1}\right)^* = \left(\frac{\beta_2}{\beta_1}\right)^{1/3} \left(\frac{b_1}{b_2}\right)^{4/3} \tag{4.19}$$

It can be seen from Equation 4.19 that the equilibrium price ratio $(p_2/p_1)^*$ depends on the ratio of utility attrition rates (β_2/β_1) and the ratio of productivity parameters (b_1/b_2). As one might expect from experience, the equilibrium price ratio $(p_2/p_1)^*$ is higher if Good 2 has a relatively high utility attrition rate (i.e. is relatively desirable to households) or a relatively low productivity (i.e. is relatively hard for firms to produce).

Substituting the equilibrium price ratio $(p_2/p_1)^*$ into Equation 4.5 or Equation 4.18 yields the equilibrium ratio of output quantities $(q_2/q_1)^*$, that is, the output quantities for which demand is equal to supply:

$$\left(\frac{q_2}{q_1}\right)^* = \left(\frac{\beta_2}{\beta_1}\right)^{1/3}\left(\frac{b_2}{b_1}\right)^{2/3} \tag{4.20}$$

These expressions (for Good 1 and Good 2) are identical to Equation 3.13, the first-order conditions (in terms of the quantity of each good) for the case of a non-monetary economy.

1.4. The Income Distribution Principle Under Profit Maximization and Derivation of the Labor Supply Curve

A household's total income (I) consists of wage income $(W=wT_L)$ received in exchange for time worked (T_L), fixed costs $(\overline{C})$, and profits (P), and can therefore be expressed as follows:

$$I = wT_L + (P + \overline{C}) \tag{4.21}$$

In order to examine the income distribution principle for the case of profit-maximizing firms, we substitute the first-order condition for profit maximization Equation 4.15 into the profit function for each production division Equation 4.14, which gives (after rearranging):

$$P_i + \overline{C}_i = \frac{p_i^2 b_i^2}{4w} \tag{4.22}$$

Squaring both sides of Equation 4.15 and dividing by b_i^2 gives the following:

$$(q_i/b_i)^2 = \frac{p_i^2 b_i^2}{4w^2} \tag{4.23}$$

Equations 4.22 and 4.23 show that (maximized) profits for Good i are distributed in accordance with $P_i + \overline{C}_i = w(q_i/b_i)^2$. Summing across the two production divisions gives:

$$P + \overline{C} = w\{(q_1 / b_1)^2 + (q_2 / b_2)^2\} \tag{4.24}$$

Given the production function $q_i = b_i T_{Li}^{1/2}$ and the definition $T_L = T_{L1} + T_{L2}$, the budget constraint can be expressed in quantity terms as $(q_1/b_1)^2 + (q_2/b_2)^2 = T_L$. Substituting this constraint into Equation 4.24 gives:

$$P + \overline{C} = w T_L \tag{4.25}$$

Substituting Equation 4.25 into Equation 4.21 then gives:

$$I = 2 w T_L \tag{4.26}$$

In other words, the distribution of profits to households by profit-maximizing firms results in households having total income (I) that is equal to twice their wage income ($W = w T_L$).

A household's labor supply function can be derived by eliminating I from Equations 4.12 and 4.26:

$$w / p_1 = (1 / 2 a \varepsilon)\{\beta_1^{1/2} + (p_2 / p_1)^{1/2} \beta_2^{1/2}\}^2 \frac{\{(T - l) - T_L\}^{3/2}}{T_L^2} \tag{4.27}$$

Figure 4.4 shows the household's labor supply function Equation 4.27 under the assumption that the price ratio p_2/p_1 remains constant. It can be seen that the labor supply curve is downward-sloping to the right.

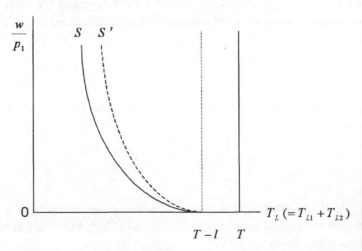

Figure 4.4 Household's labor supply function

An increase in the desirability of the consumption goods—modeled as an increase in the utility attrition rates β_1 and β_2—causes the second bracketed term on the right-hand side of Equation 4.27 to increase, such that the labor supply curve undergoes an upward shift, implying that the household is prepared to supply a greater amount of labor (T_L) for the same real wage (w/p_1).

1.5. Labor Market Equilibrium

Equation 4.17 (in Section 1.2 of this chapter) describes the relationship between the real wage w/p_1 and the amount of labor demanded by a firm:

$$w/p_1 = \frac{\left\{ b_1^2 + (p_2/p_1)^2 b_2^2 \right\}^{1/2}}{2T_L^{1/2}} \tag{4.17}$$

Equation 4.27 (in the previous section of this chapter) describes the relationship between the real wage w/p_1 and the amount of labor supplied by a household:

$$w/p_1 = (1/2a\varepsilon)\left\{ \beta_1^{1/2} + (p_2/p_1)^{1/2} \beta_2^{1/2} \right\}^2 \frac{\left\{ (T-l) - T_L \right\}^{3/2}}{T_L^2} \tag{4.27}$$

The equilibrium amount of work time T_L^* and the equilibrium real wage $(w/p_1)^*$ can be found by substituting the equilibrium price ratio (as given by Equation 4.19) for the price ratio p_2/p_1 in Equations 4.17 (the labor demand curve) and 4.27 (the labor supply curve), solving these two equations simultaneously, and rearranging:[2]

$$T_L^* = \frac{(\beta_1/b_1)^{2/3} + (\beta_2/b_2)^{2/3}}{(\beta_1/b_1)^{2/3} + (\beta_2/b_2)^{2/3} + (a\varepsilon)^{2/3}} (T-l) \tag{4.28}$$

$$(w/p_1)^* = \left\{ \frac{(\beta_1/b_1)^{2/3} + (\beta_2/b_2)^{2/3} + (a\varepsilon)^{2/3}}{(\beta_1/b_1)^{2/3}} \right\}^{1/2} \frac{b_1}{2(T-l)^{1/2}} \tag{4.29}$$

Figure 4.5 combines Figure 4.1 and Figure 4.4 to show the labor market equilibrium. The equilibrium real wage $(w/p_1)^*$ and the equilibrium amount of work time T_L^* are determined by the intersection of the labor supply curve (S) and the labor demand curve (D), shown as e in Figure 4.5.

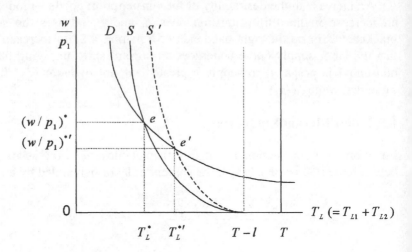

Figure 4.5 Labor market equilibrium

In a perfectly competitive economy (that is, one that has large numbers of households and firms and satisfies various other conditions), a real wage higher than the equilibrium real wage $(w/p_1)^*$ would cause the supply of labor to exceed demand, and competition between households would ensure that the real wage was bid down to the equilibrium level. Similarly, a real wage lower than the equilibrium real wage $(w/p_1)^*$ would cause demand for labor to exceed supply, and competition between firms would ensure that the real wage rose to the equilibrium level. This so-called "Walrasian price adjustment process" ensures that the equilibrium denoted by e in Figure 4.5 is stable.

Equation 4.28 is identical to Equation 3.19, the "basic equation of labor" that we derived in Chapter 3 for the case of a non-monetary economy. In other words, our "basic equation of labor" applies even in a monetary economy where households (consumers) and firms (producers) act as independent entities and where the exchange of labor and goods is mediated via the exchange of money, which implies human (household) desire can be viewed as a *universal* driver of demand and production behavior.

Let us now consider how the equilibrium levels of the real wage and employment (work time) are affected by changes in the parameters governing households and firms in the labor market.

Suppose that the desire of households for each of the consumption goods increases, as modeled by an increase in β_1 and β_2. In Figure 4.5, this causes the labor supply curve to shift (upwards) from S to S' and the equilibrium to shift from e to e', such that the equilibrium real wage

$(w/p_1)^*$ falls and the equilibrium amount of work time T_L^* rises. Similarly, if the consumption goods become less desirable to households, as modeled by a decrease in β_1 and β_2, then the labor supply curve will shift downwards, the equilibrium real wage $(w/p_1)^*$ will rise, and the equilibrium amount of work time T_L^* will fall.

Now suppose that the labor productivity parameters b_1 and b_2 increase as a result of an increase in the capital stock or some other change. In Figure 4.6, this causes the labor demand curve to shift (upwards) from D to D' and the equilibrium to shift from e to e', such that the equilibrium real wage $(w/p_1)^*$ rises and the equilibrium amount of work time T_L^* falls. Similarly, a decline in these productivity parameters causes the labor demand curve to shift downwards, such that the equilibrium real wage $(w/p_1)^*$ falls and the equilibrium amount of work time T_L^* rises.

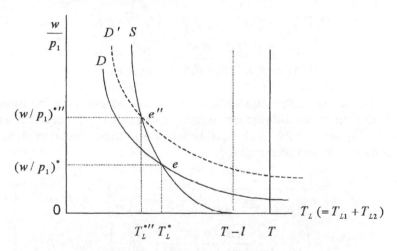

Figure 4.6 Change in labor productivity and its impact on the labor market equilibrium

The above increase in demand for labor was brought about as a result of an increase in the capital stock or some other change in technological conditions, but it is also possible that firms could ask their employees (households) to supply more labor for the same real wage in response to an increase in demand for goods or as part of a drive to launch new products. If households believe that such a request is reasonable, then they may decide to enter into a labor agreement whereby they commit to working longer hours ("overtime"). This decision by firms to increase their demand for labor would effectively cause the household labor supply curve to shift upwards as shown in Figure 4.5, such that the equilibrium real wage $(w/p_1)^*$ would fall and the equilibrium amount of work time T_L^* would rise. The increase in the β_1 and β_2 that would come about as a result of this shift in the labor supply curve can be understood in terms of an increase in real income as a result of longer working hours, i.e. an increase in the rate of "monetary utility attrition".

1.6. Framework for Simultaneous Determination of Output Quantities and Resource Allocation

In Section 1.1 of this chapter we derived Equation 4.6, which shows output quantities for each good for a given level of total household income (I). Substituting Equation 4.26 ($I=2wT_L$) into Equation 4.6 yields the following:

$$\left.\begin{array}{l} q_1 = \dfrac{1}{1+(p_2/p_1)^{1/2}(\beta_2/\beta_1)^{1/2}} 2\left(\dfrac{w}{p_1}\right)T_L \\[4mm] q_2 = \dfrac{(p_2/p_1)^{1/2}(\beta_2/\beta_1)^{1/2}}{1+(p_2/p_1)^{1/2}(\beta_2/\beta_1)^{1/2}} 2\left(\dfrac{w}{p_1}\right)\left(\dfrac{p_1}{p_2}\right)T_L \end{array}\right\} \quad (4.30)$$

Equilibrium output quantities for each good can then be found by substituting the equilibrium price ratio Equation 4.19, the equilibrium real wage Equation 4.29, and equilibrium work time Equation 4.28 into Equation 4.30 and rearranging:

$$\left.\begin{array}{l} q_1^* = \left\{\dfrac{(\beta_1/b_1)^{2/3}}{(\beta_1/b_1)^{2/3}+(\beta_2/b_2)^{2/3}+(a\varepsilon)^{2/3}}\right\}^{1/2} b_1(T-l)^{1/2} \\[5mm] q_2^* = \left\{\dfrac{(\beta_2/b_2)^{2/3}}{(\beta_1/b_1)^{2/3}+(\beta_2/b_2)^{2/3}+(a\varepsilon)^{2/3}}\right\}^{1/2} b_2(T-l)^{1/2} \end{array}\right\} \quad (4.31)$$

Given the production functions $q_i = b_i T_{Li}^{1/2}$, the equilibrium levels of work time for each good can be expressed as follows:

$$\left.\begin{array}{l} T_{L1}^* = \dfrac{(\beta_1/b_1)^{2/3}}{(\beta_1/b_1)^{2/3}+(\beta_2/b_2)^{2/3}+(a\varepsilon)^{2/3}}(T-l) \\[5mm] T_{L2}^* = \dfrac{(\beta_2/b_2)^{2/3}}{(\beta_1/b_1)^{2/3}+(\beta_2/b_2)^{2/3}+(a\varepsilon)^{2/3}}(T-l) \end{array}\right\} \quad (4.32)$$

Equations 4.31 and 4.32 are the same as Equations 3.21 and 3.22, which we derived in Chapter 3 for the case of a non-monetary economy. Furthermore, the equilibrium levels of work time for each good (Equation 4.32) determine both the total level of employment (work time) and the optimal allocation of resources (production factors), thereby completing our framework for the simultaneous determination of output quantities and resource allocation.

1.7. Household Savings and Determination of Pure Investment

We next consider pure investment under a scenario where households invest their savings (S_w) rather than setting aside that portion of their income as a means of deferring consumption.

Household savings are defined as $S_w=(1-a)I$, where a denotes the household's average propensity to consume. Equation 4.26 ($I=2wT_L$) can then be used to express household savings as:

$$S_W = 2(1-a)wT_L^*$$ (4.33)

If we use q_3^{IP} to denote output of (or demand for) the pure investment good (Good 3) and p_3 to denote the price for which it is sold, then pure investment I_P can be expressed in monetary terms as follows:

$$I_P = p_3 q_3^{IP}$$ (4.34)

In the case where firms use *all* household savings to fund pure investment I_P, i.e. where $S_w=I_P$, we can obtain the following expression from Equations 4.33 and 4.34:

$$w / p_3 = q_3^{IP} / 2(1-a)T_L^*$$ (4.35)

Equation 4.35 shows the relationship between the real wage measured in terms of the price of Good 3 (w/p_3) and the quantity of Good 3 that is produced (demanded) for a given (equilibrium) level of work time T_L^* and an economy where savings is equal to investment ($S_w=I_P$). In other words, Equation 4.35 can be viewed as the demand curve for the pure investment good under a scenario where household savings S_w are invested with firms.

As with the two consumption goods (Goods 1 and 2), the supply curve for the pure investment good (Good 3) under the assumption of profit maximization by firms can be written as follows:

$$w / p_3 = \frac{b_3^2}{2q_3^{IP}}$$ (4.36)

The equilibrium levels of the real wage $(w/p_3)^*$ and output of the pure investment good q_3^{IP*} can then be found by simultaneously solving Equations 4.35 and 4.36:

$$(w/p_3)^* = b_3 / \left\{ 2(1-a)^{1/2} (T_L^*)^{1/2} \right\} \tag{4.37}$$

$$q_3^{IP*} = b_3 (1-a)^{1/2} (T_L^*)^{1/2}$$

$$= b_3 (1-a)^{1/2} \left\{ \frac{(\beta_1/b_1)^{2/3} + (\beta_2/b_2)^{2/3}}{(\beta_1/b_1)^{2/3} + (\beta_2/b_2)^{2/3} + (a\varepsilon)^{2/3}} \right\}^{1/2} (T-l)^{1/2} \tag{4.38}$$

Figure 4.7 shows the demand Equation 4.35 and supply Equation 4.36 curves for the pure investment good. The intersection of these curves (point e) represents the production equilibrium.

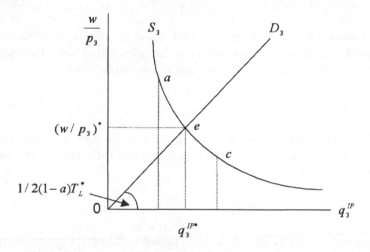

Figure 4.7 Production equilibrium

An increase in the equilibrium level of employment T_L^* would cause the slope of the demand curve $1/2(1-a)T_L^*$ to decrease, such that the equilibrium output level q_3^{IP*} would increase and the equilibrium real wage $(w/p_3)^*$ would fall. Similarly, a decrease in the equilibrium level of employment T_L^* would cause the equilibrium output level q_3^{IP*} to fall and the equilibrium real wage $(w/p_3)^*$ to rise.

1.8. The Supply-Demand Adjustment Process for Pure Investment Goods

We next consider the adjustment process in cases where firms' desired level of pure investment (i.e. their demand for corporate savings) is not equal to the supply of household savings.

Suppose that firms' desired level of pure investment is less than the supply of household savings, i.e. $I_P < S_W$. From Equations 4.33 and 4.34, this implies that $w/p_3 > \{1/2(1-a)T_L^*\}q_3^{IP}$, such that the combination of w/p_3 and q_3^{IP} lies above the demand curve D_3 and to the left (for example, at point a on the supply curve S_3 in Figure 4.7). In this case, firms' desired level of pure investment q_3^{IP} is less than the equilibrium level of pure investment q_3^{IP*} at which pure investment is equal to household savings, such that a portion of household savings is not demanded by firms. However, this state of affairs would trigger competition among households with regard to the interest rate demanded from firms (in that households would be prepared to accept lower interest rates), and this competition would continue for as long as the level of household savings remained higher than the desired level of pure investment. As a result, the desire (willingness) of firms to undertake pure investment would gradually improve to the point where the desired level of pure investment would equal the supply of household savings.

Now suppose that firms' desired level of pure investment is higher than the supply of household savings, i.e. $I_P > S_W$. From Equations 4.33 and 4.34, this implies that $w/p_3 < \{1/2(1-a)T_L^*\}q_3^{IP}$, such that the combination of w/p_3 and q_3^{IP} lies below the demand curve D_3 and to the right (for example, at point c on the supply curve S_3 in Figure 4.7). In this case, firms' desired level of pure investment q_3^{IP} is greater than the equilibrium level of pure investment q_3^{IP*} at which pure investment is equal to household savings, such that household savings are not sufficient to finance the desired level of pure investment. However, this state of affairs would trigger competition among firms with regard to the interest rate offered to households (in that firms would be prepared to offer higher interest rates), and this competition would continue for as long as the level of household savings remained lower than the desired level of pure investment. As a result, the desire (willingness) of firms to undertake pure investment would gradually diminish to the point where the desired level of pure investment would equal the supply of household savings.

It should be clear from the above that interest rate adjustments in the lending market will serve to correct any initial imbalance between demand for household savings (the desired level of pure investment) and the supply of household savings.

2. Introduction of Monetary Elements and Completion of Our Framework

In this section we add monetary elements to our model based on utility attrition (human desire), and complete our theoretical framework for analysis of a monetary economy by incorporating a mechanism—similar to that used in classical macroeconomic theory—for the determination of interest rates and price levels (money wages).

2.1. The Loanable Funds Theory and Determination of Interest Rates

In this book, we consider pure investment as part of a framework where households invest their savings (S_w) rather than setting aside that portion of their income as a means of deferring consumption, and where firms issue bonds and/or shares in order to gain access to the entire amount of these savings, which they then use to finance new investment (pure investment). This framework is similar to the "loanable funds theory" of (traditional) classical macroeconomic theory.

The loanable funds theory focuses on how firms raise the cash flow that they require in order to undertake pure investment, and argues that the interest rate adjusts so that the supply of investment funds (in the form of household savings) is equal to the level of investment spending undertaken by firms. In this book we follow a similar approach regarding the determination of the interest rate.

We begin by considering the supply side of the loan market. Household savings (S_w) can be expressed in terms of the equilibrium output level for the pure investment good Equation 4.38.

We next consider the demand side of the loan market. According to John Maynard Keynes (1936), the pure investment that is funded by loans is undertaken to the point where the marginal efficiency of capital (which diminishes as the level of investment increases) is equal to the interest rate (r) for given supply prices of machinery and other equipment and a given stream of expected future earnings $(Q_t^e$, where the subscript t denotes the investment horizon). An increase in Q_t^e causes the marginal efficiency of capital (MEC) curve to shift upwards, such that a higher level of pure investment is undertaken for a given interest rate. In other words, pure investment is an increasing function of Q_t^e, the stream of expected future earnings. As such, the pure investment function may be written as $q_3^{IP} = q_3^{IP}(Q_t^e, r)$, where $dq_3^{IP}/dQ_t^e > 0$ and $dq_3^{IP}/dr < 0$. An increase in Q_t^e, is likely to stem from an increase in households' desire for consumption goods, and we have therefore decided to replace Q_t^e with

β_1/ε, the relative utility attrition rate for Good 1 (the reference good), such that the firm's pure investment function can be written as follows:

$$q_3^{IP} = q_3^{IP}(\beta_1 / \varepsilon, r) \tag{4.39}$$

where $dq_3^{IP} / d(\beta_1 / \varepsilon) > 0$ and $dq_3^{IP} / dr < 0$

We now assume that the firm's pure investment function is additively separable, using q_{31}^{IP} to denote the component that depends on the relative utility attrition rate, q_{32}^{IP} to denote the component that depends on the interest rate, and $\overline{q_3}$ to denote the component that depends on other (independent) factors, such that:

$$q_3^{IP} = q_{31}^{IP}(\beta_1 / \varepsilon) + q_{32}^{IP}(r) + \overline{q_3} \tag{4.40}$$

where $dq_{31}^{IP} / d(\beta_1 / \varepsilon) > 0$ and $dq_{32}^{IP} / dr < 0$

We also assume that q_{31}^{IP} and q_{32}^{IP} are linear functions that may be written as $q_{31}^{IP} = \mu\beta_1/\varepsilon$ and $q_{32}^{IP} = h - \rho r$ (where μ, h, and ρ are positive constants), such that the pure investment function may be written as:

$$q_3^{IP} = (\overline{q_3} + h) + \mu\beta_1 / \varepsilon - \rho\, r \tag{4.41}$$

Under the assumption that demand for loans is equal to the supply of loans, the equilibrium interest rate (termed the "natural interest rate" by Knut Wicksell) can be determined by eliminating q_3^{IP} from Equations 4.38 and 4.41:

$$r = \frac{1}{\rho}\left\{(\overline{q_3} + h) + \mu\beta_1 / \varepsilon - b_3(1-a)^{1/2}(T_L^*)^{1/2}\right\} \tag{4.42}$$

Recall that T_L^* denotes the equilibrium level of work time (employment) from Equation 4.28.

We next consider currency creation by a banking system (ΔM) as a supply-side factor in the loans market and the net increase in the currency holdings of households and firms (ΔL) as a demand-side factor in the loans market, and look at how the interest rate is determined.

Currency creation by a banking system can be expressed in volume terms as $\Delta M/p_3$ (that is, by dividing it by the price of the pure investment good). Adding this to Equation 4.38 gives q_S^{IP}, the supply of (new) pure investment goods. Similarly, adding $\Delta L/p_3$ to Equation 4.41 gives q_D^{IP}, the demand for (new) pure investment goods. Under the assumption that demand for pure investment goods (q_D^{IP}) is equal to the supply of pure investment goods (q_S^{IP}), the equilibrium interest rate (termed the "market interest rate" (r_m) by Knut Wicksell) can be determined as follows:

$$r_m = \frac{1}{\rho}\left\{(\overline{q_3}+h)+\mu\beta_1 / \varepsilon+(\varDelta L-\varDelta M)/ p_3 -b_3(1-a)^{1/2}(T_L^*)^{1/2}\right\} \quad (4.43)$$

2.2. The Relationship Between the Utility Attrition Rate and the Money Supply

In this section we consider the relationship between the utility attrition rate and the money supply by way of preparation for a discussion (in Section 2.3) of price level determination based on the quantity theory of money (the so-called "transactions version" of the quantity equation).

According to the theory of credit creation, the money supply (M) is defined as the sum of cash currency (C) and deposit currency (D) held by the private sector excluding banks (i.e. households, firms, etc.), while the central bank's obligations to the private sector ("high-powered money", denoted by H) is defined as the sum of banknotes in circulation (equal to C, cash currency held by the private sector excluding banks) and private-sector banks' cash reserves (R). Given that $M=C+D$ and $H=C+R$, the following relationship applies between the money supply and high-powered money:

$$M = \frac{cc+1}{cc+re} H \qquad\qquad (4.44)$$

Here cc is equal to C/D (the ratio of the private sector's cash currency holdings to its deposit currency holdings) and re is equal to R/D (the ratio of private-sector banks' cash reserves to their deposits).

The constant $(cc+1)/(cc+re)$ in Equation 4.44 is known as the "credit multiplier" or "money multiplier", and measures the dollar amount by which the money supply increases (including secondary deposits that arise as a result of lending by private-sector banks) as a result of a $1 increase in the amount of high-powered money supplied by the central bank.

Equation 4.44 is based on the assumption that all of the secondary deposits that arise as a result of lending (with the exception of cash reserves) are used actively for lending purposes, but this will not necessarily apply if banks are proactive in managing credit risk. In other words, banks may use funds in one of two ways: (1) "active investment", where banks seek returns in exchange for taking on the credit risk associated with borrowers; and (2) "defensive investment", in which banks emphasize safety over returns. When the economy is in a downturn and banks believe that default risk has increased, economic agents may give a greater priority to defensive investment. For banks this may mean investing a greater proportion of funds in government bonds or other securities with an extremely low risk of default, while firms may demand money to meet the so-called "precautionary motive" (for example, firms may prepare for future uncertainty by raising cash for future loan repayments or to meet increased calls for cash settlement from suppliers). Both types of behavior cause the money multiplier to decline, either because banks channel funds into securities markets by purchasing bonds or shares, or because cash remains with banks in the form of firms' (precautionary) cash currency deposits that cannot be used to fund other lending activity. However, in this section we assume that cash does not remain dormant at banks for an extended period of time, and that cash entering the securities markets remains in circulation as a result of trading in other securities.

If we use λ to denote the proportion of available funds (excluding cash reserves) that is "actively" invested, such that $(1-\lambda)$ denotes the proportion of available funds that is "defensively" invested, then the relationship between the money supply and high-powered money (taking into account the investment behavior of the banking system) can be written as follows:[3]

$$M = \frac{cc+1}{cc+1-(1-re)\lambda} H \qquad (4.45)$$

If we assume that cc (the ratio of the private sector's cash currency holdings to its deposit currency holdings), re (the ratio of private-sector banks' cash reserves to their deposits), and H (high-powered money) are constants, then Equation 4.45 shows that the money supply (M) is an increasing function of the proportion of actively-invested funds (λ). This relationship is shown in Figure 4.8.

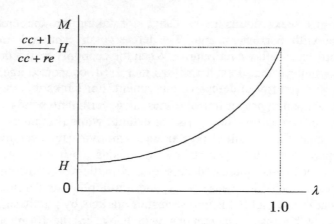

Figure 4.8 Relationship between the proportion of actively-invested funds
(λ) and the money supply (M) under the condition that high-
powered money and other parameters remain constant

In determining λ (the proportion of funds that is to be actively invested), the banking system—which obviously places a high priority on the recoverability of loaned funds—is likely to monitor trends relating to corporate income (profits). Corporate profits are proportional to the equilibrium level of output (or employment), which is an increasing function of the relative utility attrition rate β_1/ε. As such, the money supply M can be expressed as an increasing function of β_1/ε, the relative utility attrition rate for Good 1 (the reference good).[4]

The increase in the money supply (M) that results from an increase in the relative utility attrition rate (β_1/ε) is independent of the increase in total output (in volume terms) that results from an increase in the relative utility attrition rate (β_1/ε): the latter results from the independent behavior of households and firms, while the former results from the independent behavior of the banking system (the third sector of the economy). In other words, the two phenomena arise as a result of rational behavior on the part of different economic agents.

2.3. The Quantity Theory of Money and the Determination of Price and Money Wage Levels

We next consider how the price of the reference good (the price level) and the level of the money wage are determined, employing a framework that is based on the quantity theory of money (the so-called "transactions version" of the quantity equation) from classical macroeconomic theory. This approach focuses on the transactional exchange of money, and argues that the price level is determined by the relationship whereby the total value of transactions during a given period of time is equal to the money supply at the start of that period multiplied by the average number of times that money passes from buyer to seller (the so-called "velocity of money").

If the money supply at the beginning of (and throughout) a given period of time is denoted by M and the velocity of money is denoted by V, then the "transactions version" of the quantity equation for a two-good model can be written as:

$$MV = p_1 q_1 + p_2 q_2$$
$$= p_1 \left(q_1 + \frac{p_2}{p_1} q_2 \right)$$

Equation 4.46 is obtained by substituting the equilibrium output levels (from Equation 4.31) and the equilibrium price ratio (from Equation 4.19) into the above equation and rearranging:

$$MV = p_1 b_1 \left\{ 1 + \left(\frac{\beta_2}{\beta_1} \right)^{2/3} \left(\frac{b_1}{b_2} \right)^{2/3} \right\}^{1/2} T_L^{1/2} \tag{4.46}$$

This implies that the relationship between the price level (the price of the reference good, p_1) and the employment level is as follows:

$$p_1 = \frac{MV}{b_1 \left\{ 1 + (\beta_2 / \beta_1)^{2/3} (b_1 / b_2)^{2/3} \right\}^{1/2} T_L^{1/2}} \tag{4.47}$$

The relationship between the relative utility attrition rate (β_1/ε) and the money supply, taking into account the independent behavior of the banking system as discussed in the previous section, can be expressed as follows:

$$M = \frac{cc + 1}{cc + 1 - (1 - re)\lambda(\beta_1 / \varepsilon)} H \tag{4.48}$$
$$= M(\beta_1 / \varepsilon, cc, re, H)$$

Once again, cc is equal to C/D (the ratio of the private sector's cash currency holdings to its deposit currency holdings), re is equal to R/D (the ratio of private-sector banks' cash reserves to their deposits), and H denotes high-powered money.

Substituting Equation 4.48 into Equation 4.47 yields the following relationship between the price level (the price of the reference good, p_1) and the employment level (T_L):

$$p_1 = \frac{M(\beta_1/\varepsilon, cc, re, H)V}{b_1\left\{1+(\beta_2/\beta_1)^{2/3}(b_1/b_2)^{2/3}\right\}^{1/2} T_L^{1/2}} \qquad (4.49)$$

where $\partial M / \partial(\beta_1/\varepsilon) > 0$, $\partial M / \partial cc < 0$, $\partial M / \partial re < 0$, and $\partial M / \partial H > 0$

The relationship between p_1 and T_L described in Equation 4.49 was derived using the quantity theory of money (the so-called "transactions version" of the quantity equation) while allowing for the independent behavior of the banking system. In this book, we refer to Equation 4.49 as the "aggregate demand function" (expressed in terms of the employment level), as it describes the combinations of price levels (p_1) and employment levels (or purchasable quantities of goods) that arise as a result of credit creation by banks and its impact on a society's purchasing power.

The equilibrium employment level (T_L^*) is determined in the labor market irrespective of developments in the money market. As such, we refer to the function describing T_L^* (which is parallel to the price axis) as the "aggregate supply function" (expressed in terms of the employment level).

The price level (the price of the reference good, p_1) is determined by the intersection of the aggregate demand function and the aggregate supply function, and can be expressed as follows:

$$p_1^* = \frac{M(\beta_1/\varepsilon, cc, re, H)V}{b_1\left\{1+(\beta_2/\beta_1)^{2/3}(b_1/b_2)^{2/3}\right\}^{1/2} (T_L^*)^{1/2}} \qquad (4.50)$$

where T_L^* is the equilibrium work time (employment level) from Equation 4.28.

The equilibrium money wage is determined by multiplying the price of the reference good from Equation 4.50 by the equilibrium real wage from Equation 4.29:

$$w^* = \frac{M(\beta/\varepsilon, cc, re, H)V}{2T_L^*} \qquad (4.51)$$

Figure 4.9 shows the money market equilibrium based on the aggregate demand function (AD) and the aggregate supply function (AS), both of which are expressed in terms of the employment level.

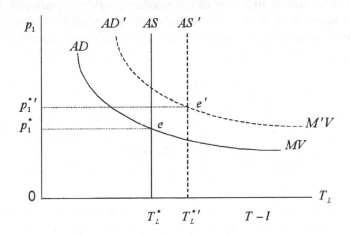

Figure 4.9 Money market equilibrium based on the aggregate demand function (AD) and the aggregate supply function (AS)

In Figure 4.9, T_L^* denotes the equilibrium employment level corresponding to the initial relative utility attrition rate (β_1/ε) and M denotes the money supply (such that the amount of money circulating among economic agents is MV). This corresponds to an initial price level of p_1^*, which is determined by the intersection (at point e) of the vertical line passing through T_L^* (AS) and the hyperbola based on MV (AD). If the relative utility attrition rate (β_1/ε) increases, then the amount of money circulating among economic agents and the employment level will both increase, to $M'V$ and $T_L^{*\prime}$ respectively. As a result, the price of the reference good would increase to $p_1^{*\prime}$, as determined by the intersection (at point e') of the vertical line passing through $T_L^{*\prime}$ (AS') and the hyperbola based on $M'V$ (AD').

3. Measurability of the Utility Attrition Rate

In order to use our theoretical framework to analyze macroeconomic variables such as employment and output, we must be able to measure (at least) the utility attrition rates β_1 and β_2 and the leisure utility parameter ε. In this section, we show how these utility parameters can be measured in practice.

3.1. Measuring the Utility Attrition Rate

Equation 4.5 gives the first-order condition for maximization of expected utility from goods in a monetary economy, while Equation 4.28 is our "basic equation of labor". We reproduce these equations below (including the proportion of output allocated to capital (θ) in Equation 4.28 as the developed solution for T_L^*):

$$\frac{q_2}{q_1} = \left(\frac{\beta_2}{\beta_1}\right)^{1/2} \left(\frac{p_1}{p_2}\right)^{1/2} \tag{4.5}$$

$$T_L^* = \frac{(\beta_1/b_1)^{2/3} + (\beta_2/b_2)^{2/3}}{(\beta_1/b_1)^{2/3} + (\beta_2/b_2)^{2/3} + \{a(1-\theta)\varepsilon\}^{2/3}} (T-l) \tag{4.28}$$

$q_1^{c\prime} = aq_1^c = a(1-\theta)q_1$ · $q_2^{c\prime} = aq_2^c = a(1-\theta)q_2$ implies that q_2/q_1 (the ratio of output quantities) is equal to $q_2^{c\prime}/q_1^{c\prime}$ (the ratio of purchased quantities). Data on $(p_1, q_1^{c\prime})$ and $(p_2, q_2^{c\prime})$ (equilibrium prices and the quantities that are purchased at these prices) are directly observable, such that it is possible to determine the ratio of output quantities q_2/q_1 ($=q_2^{c\prime}/q_1^{c\prime}$) and the price ratio p_1/p_2. These ratios can then be substituted into Equation 4.5 to find the ratio of utility attrition rates β_2/β_1.

Dividing both the numerator and the denominator on the right-hand side of Equation 4.28 by $\beta_1^{2/3}$ yields the following:

$$T_L^* = \frac{(1/b_1)^{2/3} + (\beta_2/\beta_1)^{2/3}(1/b_2)^{2/3}}{(1/b_1)^{2/3} + (\beta_2/\beta_1)^{2/3}(1/b_2)^{2/3} + \{a(1-\theta)(\varepsilon/\beta_1)\}^{2/3}} (T-l) \tag{4.28$'$}$$

In Equation 4.28$'$, labor productivity parameters (b_1 and b_2), the average propensity to consume (a), the proportion of output allocated to capital (θ), units of time T, minimum necessary leisure time (l), and equilibrium work hours (employment) (T_L^*) are all observable or can be set arbitrarily, and the ratio of utility attrition rates β_2/β_1 can be determined as discussed above. Substituting the relevant values for these variables into Equation 4.28$'$ produces a value for ε/β_1, the reciprocal of which is equal to β_1/ε, the relative utility attrition rate for Good 1. This can then be multiplied by the ratio of utility attrition rates β_2/β_1 in order to determine β_2/ε, the relative utility attrition rate for Good 2.

In other words, while it is not possible to determine the absolute levels of the utility attrition rates β_1 and β_2 or the leisure utility parameter ε, it is possible to measure the ratios β_1/ε and β_2/ε. Furthermore, under our assumption that the leisure utility parameter ε is stable and is not affected by work hours or other labor conditions, the relative utility attrition rates β_1/ε and β_2/ε can be used as "indices" for β_1 and β_2.

It is not possible to measure the other parameters of the utility attrition function and the leisure utility function, i.e. the initial utility levels (α_1 and α_2) and the parameter that denotes the upper bound for the level of utility from leisure (γ). However, this does not represent a significant problem, as these parameters are eliminated during the process of deriving our "basic equation of labor" Equation (4.28).

It should be clear from the above discussion that it is not necessary to measure all of the parameters of the utility attrition function and the leisure utility function (that is, these functions need not be fully specified), and that analysis based on our theoretical framework is possible provided that *relative* utility attrition rates can be determined as ratios of parameters that are not directly observable.

3.2. A Simple Worked Example

We now consider a simple macroeconomic example for a monetary economy based on observations over a given period of time (T).

Assumptions:
(1) The representative household (consumer/worker) has a linear utility attrition function and maximizes expected total utility (the sum of expected utility from goods and utility of leisure).
(2) Firms produce two goods (which function both as consumption goods and renewal investment goods) based on production functions $q_i = b_i T_{Li}^{1/2}$.
(3) Firms undertake pure investment that is equal to household savings in monetary terms.
(4) There is no capital attrition, and the proportion (of output) allocated to capital (θ) is zero.

Observed data:
- Total production Y: \$5.0 billion
- Household consumption C_w: \$3.645 billion
- Equilibrium prices and output levels for each consumption good:

$$\text{Good 1: } (p_1, q_1^{c\,\prime}) = (\frac{12{,}500}{36} \text{ \$}, \frac{314{,}928}{60} \text{ thousand units})$$

$$\text{Good 2: } (p_2, q_2^{c\,\prime}) = (600 \text{ \$}, \frac{182{,}250}{60} \text{ thousand units})$$

- Production functions for each consumption/renewal investment good (per household):

Good 1: $q_1 = \dfrac{1,000}{125} T_{L1}^{1/2}$

Good 2: $q_2 = \dfrac{1,000}{216} T_{L2}^{1/2}$

- Number of households: 100,000 (labor force participation rate: 100%)
- Equilibrium work hours (employment) per household T_L^*: 7.5/24 × T
- Minimum necessary leisure time per household l: 6.9/24 × T

Calculations:

(1) The ratio of utility attrition rates for the representative household (β_2/β_1):

From $q_1^{c\prime}=a(1-\theta)q_1$ and $q_2^{c\prime}=a(1-\theta)q_2$, we obtain $q_2/q_1=q_2^{c\prime}/q_1^{c\prime}$. We can then substitute data on observed equilibrium prices and output (sale) amounts into the first-order condition for maximization of expected utility from goods Equation 4.5 as follows:

$$\frac{182,250,000/60}{314,928,000/60} = \left(\frac{\beta_2}{\beta_1}\right)^{1/2} \left(\frac{12,500/36}{600}\right)^{1/2} \quad \therefore \frac{\beta_2}{\beta_1} = \frac{125}{216} \quad \text{(A-1)}$$

(2) Total household income (I)/average propensity to consume (a):

The relationship between total domestic production (gross domestic product) Y and total household income I is $I=(1-\theta)Y$. Here the proportion of output allocated to capital (θ) is zero, such that $I=Y$. This implies that $I=\$5.0$ billion.

The average propensity to consume (a) is equal to C_W divided by I, such that:

$$a = \frac{C_W}{I} = \frac{\$3.645 billion}{\$5.0 billion} = \frac{729}{1,000} (=0.729) \quad \text{(A-2)}$$

(3) Ratio of work time to total disposable time ($T_L/T-l$):

$$\frac{T_L}{T-l} = \frac{T_L}{T}\frac{T}{T-l} = \frac{7.5}{24} \times \frac{24}{24-6.9} = \frac{25}{57} \quad \text{(A-3)}$$

(4) The household's relative utility attrition rates for each good (β_1/ε, β_2/ε):

Divide both sides of Equation 4.28′ by ($T-l$), and then substitute data on the labor productivity parameters b_1 and b_2 and previous results (A-1), (A-2) and (A-3) to yield:

$$\frac{25}{57} = \frac{(125/1,000)^{2/3} + (216/1,000)^{2/3}(125/216)^{2/3}}{(125/1,000)^{2/3} + (216/1,000)^{2/3}(125/216)^{2/3} + (729/1,000)^{2/3}(\varepsilon/\beta_1)^{2/3}}$$

Solving this yields:

$$\frac{\varepsilon}{\beta_1} = \frac{512}{729} = 0.702 \quad \therefore \frac{\beta_1}{\varepsilon} = \frac{729}{512} = 1.424$$

Also:

$$\frac{\beta_2}{\varepsilon} = \frac{\beta_2}{\beta_1}\frac{\beta_1}{\varepsilon} = \frac{125}{216}\frac{729}{512} = 0.824$$

NOTES

1. If we apply $\tau_1 = T / q_1$ and $\tau_2 = T / q_2$ to Equation 4.5 and rearranging, we obtain the following equation and its numerators are equal to the time-integral of diminished utility which is determined by the utility attrition function $U_i(t) = \alpha_i - \beta_i t$ and a reconsumption cycle of τ_i $(i = 1,2)$.

$$\frac{(1/2)\beta_1\tau_1^2}{p_1} = \frac{(1/2)\beta_2\tau_2^2}{p_2}$$

Therefore "The Law of Equi-marginal Utility" is replaced by a new law which requires the equality of the ratio of time-integral of diminished utility to the price of goods.

2. This calculation is somewhat complicated, but can be simplified by setting $1 + (\beta_2 / \beta_1)^{2/3}(b_1 / b_2)^{2/3} = A$ after substituting the equilibrium price ratio (as given by Equation 4.19 into Equations 4.17 and 4.27.

3. The sum of an infinite sequence with initial term H and common factor $(1-re)\lambda / (cc+1)$.

4. The relationship between corporate income (profits) and equilibrium production (employment) is discussed in Chapter 8, Section 2.

Chapter 5

Human Psychology and Economic Fluctuation

Our analysis in the previous chapters has assumed: (1) that pure investment undertaken by firms during a given period of time has no impact on utility attrition rates or labor productivity parameters for the same period; and (2) that the household's (or Robinson Crusoe's) utility attrition function for each consumption good is linear (i.e. the utility attrition rate is a constant). Based on these assumptions—which were required in order to ensure stability—we derived our "basic equation of labor", which describes the relationship between a household's (or Crusoe's) utility attrition rates and the time that it (or he) spends working. Short-run analysis based on a non-linear production technology satisfying the principle of diminishing marginal productivity yields the following equation for a two-good model:

$$T_L^* = \frac{(\beta_1 / b_1)^{2/3} + (\beta_2 / b_2)^{2/3}}{(\beta_1 / b_1)^{2/3} + (\beta_2 / b_2)^{2/3} + (a\varepsilon)^{2/3}} (T - I) \qquad (4.28)$$

Equation 4.28 (which describes the equilibrium level of employment T_L^*) was derived using static equilibrium analysis that is valid provided that the above stability assumptions hold, in which case the level of employment will be stable for the economy as a whole and economic fluctuations will not occur.

In this chapter we remove the above assumptions relating to stability with a view to analyzing dynamic fluctuations in the level of employment or output. This dynamic framework enables us to demonstrate the relationship between human psychology (desire) and economic fluctuation, which represents the main theme of this book. We also consider the role of human psychology in various phenomena such as economic growth and the creation and destruction of financial bubbles.

Assumptions Behind Our Analysis

The macroeconomic analysis in this book assumes that a household's utility attrition function for any given good is either: (a) a linear utility attrition function; or (b) a non-linear increasing-gradient utility attrition function (one for which the utility attrition rate increases with the passage of time).[1]

Certain individual households might not have any desire for a given good (corresponding to a zero utility attrition rate), and the form of the utility attrition function will obviously differ across households. For the purposes of our analysis, however, we assume that it is possible to work with "smoothed" utility attrition functions that are obtained by (vertically) adding the utility attrition functions of individual households and then dividing by the total number of households.

1. Human Psychology and the Economic Cycle

1.1. Non-Linearity of the Utility Attrition Function and the Emergence of an Economic Cycle

As stated above, for the purposes of this chapter we assume that a household's utility attrition function for any given good is either: (a) a linear utility attrition function; or (b) a non-linear increasing-gradient utility attrition function. The following table divides goods into various categories and considers the form that the utility attrition function for each category is likely to take.

Type of good	Form of utility attrition function	Notes
(1) Food and drink	Linear	Primarily attrition over time
(2) Housing (shelter)	Linear or non-linear increasing-gradient	Primarily attrition over time
(3) Clothes, footwear, expendable supplies, etc.	Linear	Primarily attrition with use
(4) Cultural activities and entertainment	Linear or non-linear increasing-gradient	Primarily attrition over time
(5) Durable consumer goods	Non-linear increasing-gradient	Primarily attrition with use

Table 5.1 Major types of goods and the forms of their utility attrition functions

Note that "durable consumer items" include motor vehicles, furniture, and electrical appliances.

Prior to the advent of capitalism, human labor productivity was extremely low, and only necessities (such as categories (1)–(3) in the above table) were traded between businesses (firms) and households, such that economic society as a whole was perhaps dominated by goods with linear utility attrition functions. If this were indeed the case, then because the utility attrition rate for a given good would have remained constant irrespective of the volume of that good that was demanded (consumed), any circumstances that caused the level of household employment to increase beyond the equilibrium level (T_L^*)—such that output of goods increased and the reconsumption cycle shortened—would have represented nothing more than a temporary shock. In other words, because utility attrition rates (β_1 and β_2) would have remained unchanged, the level of employment would soon have moved back to T_L^* in accordance with Equation 4.28.

However, the advent of capitalism, the industrial revolution that began in England, and the subsequent spread of electric power and mass production brought about massive increases in human labor productivity, and the range of goods that were traded within an economy expanded to encompass goods (and services) that would initially have been considered "luxuries" (non-essential items such as categories (4) and (5) in the above table). As a result, consumers began to have access to goods with non-linear increasing-gradient utility attrition functions, in addition to those goods with linear utility attrition functions that had previously been available. This increase in the range of goods (and hence the scope of human desire) would appear to have considerable relevance to the history of economic fluctuations since the early 19th century.

Let us now consider an economy with two consumption goods (Good 1 and Good 2) that are desired by all households. Good 1 is assumed to have a linear utility attrition function, while Good 2 is assumed to have a non-linear increasing-gradient utility attrition function. In order to simplify the subsequent analysis, we transform Equation 4.28 into the following equation:

$$T_L^* = \frac{1}{1+\dfrac{a^{2/3}}{(\beta_1/\varepsilon)^{2/3}(1/b_1)^{2/3}+(\beta_2/\varepsilon)^{2/3}(1/b_2)^{2/3}}}(T-I) \qquad (5.1)$$

We denote the initial equilibrium level of household employment by T_L^{*0} and the corresponding equilibrium output levels for Good 1 and Good 2 by q_1^0 and q_2^0 respectively. As in Section 2 of Chapter 2, we use

$\tau = T/q^C$ to denote the "reconsumption cycle" for the case where q^C acts of consumption take place during T units of time, such that the (average) household initially has reconsumption cycles of $\tau_1^0 = T/q_1^{C0} = T/aq_1^0$ and $\tau_2^0 = T/q_2^{C0} = T/aq_2^0$ for Good 1 and Good 2 respectively. The utility attrition functions for Good 1 and Good 2 are shown in Figure 5.1 (a) and (b) respectively, with the utility attrition rates that correspond to the reconsumption cycles of τ_1^0 and τ_2^0 denoted by $\beta_1^0 (=\beta_1)$ and $\beta_2^0 (=\beta_2\tau_2^0)$ respectively.

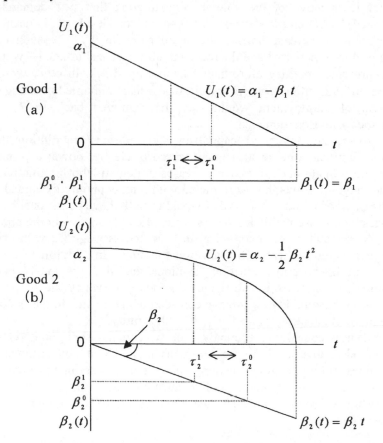

Figure 5.1 Relationship between reconsumption cycles and the utility attrition rates

If the initial equilibrium level of household employment increases from T_L^{*0} to T_L^{*1} for some reason, then the equilibrium output amounts will increase from q_1^0 to q_1^1 and from q_2^0 to q_2^1, and the reconsumption cycles will decrease (shorten) from τ_1^0 to τ_1^1 and from τ_2^0 to τ_2^1. The utility attrition rate for Good 1 (β_1) remains unchanged despite this shortening of the reconsumption cycle, but the utility attrition rate for Good 2 decreases from β_2^0 $(=\beta_2\tau_2^0)$ to β_2^1 $(=\beta_2\tau_2^1)$. This serves to reduce the parameter β_2/ε in Equation 5.1, thereby placing downward pressure on the equilibrium level of household employment (T_L^*). The equilibrium level of household employment then falls back from T_L^{*1} to T_L^{*0} as a result of this pressure, such that the equilibrium output amounts fall back from q_1^1 to q_1^0 and from q_2^1 to q_2^0, and the reconsumption cycles increase (lengthen) from τ_1^1 to τ_1^0 and from τ_2^1 to τ_2^0. The utility attrition rate for Good 1 (β_1) once again remains unchanged, but the utility attrition rate for Good 2 rises back from β_2^1 $(=\beta_2\tau_2^1)$ to β_2^0 $(=\beta_2\tau_2^0)$. This serves to increase the parameter β_2/ε in Equation 5.1, thereby placing upward pressure on the equilibrium level of household employment (T_L^*).[2]

This example demonstrates how the existence of a good with a non-linear increasing-gradient utility attrition function (an increasing utility attrition rate) is consistent with an endogenous economic cycle driven by the inverse relationship between the level of household employment (or output levels) and the utility attrition rate (the fundamental driver of demand).

We now explain the mechanism behind this endogenous economic cycle under the assumption that the types of consumption goods and production functions are given.

When the economy is improving, the reconsumption cycle (average "resting" period) for each good shortens as a result of an increase in the rate at which goods are purchased by households. In the case of Good 2, which has a non-linear increasing-gradient utility attrition function, the utility attrition rate is low immediately after the good is purchased, such that a shortening of the reconsumption cycle serves to reduce the rate at which utility declines (desire is reduced) for the economy (society) as a whole. This reduction in the (average) rate of utility attrition (the fundamental driver of demand) for Good 2 serves to reduce demand for Good 2 and thereby serves to reduce the total level of employment (output), which creates downward pressure on the economy. Once the economy enters a downturn as a result of this pressure, the reconsumption cycle (average "resting" period) for each good lengthens as a result of a decline in the rate at which goods are purchased by households. This lengthening of the reconsumption cycle means that the utility attrition rate for Good 2 is increasing for a longer period of time, and therefore serves to increase the rate at which utility declines (desire increases) for the economy (society) as a whole. This increase in the (average) rate of utility attrition (the fundamental driver of demand) for Good 2 serves to increase demand for Good 2 and thereby serves to increase the total level of employment (output), which creates upward pressure on the economy.

We now illustrate this mechanism using a simple mathematical model.
The utility attrition function for Good 2, shown in Figure 5.1 (b), is
given by $\beta_2(\tau_2)=\beta_2\tau_2=\beta_2 T/q_2^c$, which means that $d\beta_2/dq_2^c=-\beta_2 T/(q_2^c)^2$,
i.e. $d\beta_2=-\beta_2 T/(q_2^c)^2 dq_2^c$. A change in the utility attrition rate for the
current period $(d\beta_2)$ is likely to result from a change in the consumption
level (dq_2^c) at some point in the past. For the purpose of our analysis, we
assume that a change in the utility attrition rate for the current period
$(d\beta_2)$ results from a change in the consumption level (dq_2^c) in the
previous period, and rewrite the previous equation in terms of discrete
variables (i.e. as a difference equation):

$$\beta_{2t}-\beta_{2t-1}=-\beta_2 T/(q_2^c)^2(q_{2t-1}^c-q_{2t-2}^c) \tag{5.2}$$

Using the equilibrium output level for Good 2 Equation 4.31 and the
relationship $q_2^c=aq_2$, we may express q_2^c (the equilibrium level of
consumption of Good 2) as follows:

$$\begin{aligned}
q_2^c &= a\left\{\frac{(\beta_2/b_2)^{2/3}}{(\beta_1/b_1)^{2/3}+(\beta_2/b_2)^{2/3}+(a\varepsilon)^{2/3}}\right\}^{1/2} b_2(T-l)^{1/2}\\
&= a\left\{\frac{(1/b_2)^{2/3}(\beta_2/\varepsilon)^{2/3}}{(1/b_1)^{2/3}(\beta_1/\varepsilon)^{2/3}+(1/b_2)^{2/3}(\beta_2/\varepsilon)^{2/3}+a^{2/3}}\right\}^{1/2} b_2(T-l)^{1/2}
\end{aligned}$$
$$\tag{5.3}$$

Figure 5.2 shows that q_2^c (the equilibrium level of consumption of
Good 2) is a non-linear increasing function of the parameter β_2/ε.
However, it is possible to approximate this curve as a linear function over
a limited domain (such as in the circled region in Figure 5.2).

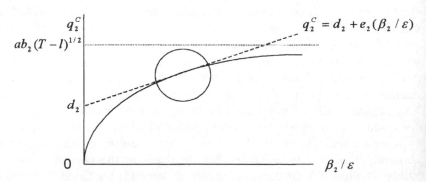

*Figure 5.2 Approximation of a non-linear increasing function as a linear
function over a limited domain*

If we write this linear approximation as $q_2^c = d_2 + e_2(\beta_2/\varepsilon)$ (where the intercept d_2 and the slope e_2 are parameters that depend on how the approximation is chosen), then we may write $dq_2^c = (e_2/\varepsilon)d\beta_2$. In this case, as we are approximating the relationship between q_2^c (the equilibrium level of consumption of Good 2) and β_2 (the utility attrition rate for Good 2) during the same period of time, dq_2^c and $d\beta_2$ represent changes that occur during the same period of time. As such, we may rewrite the previous equation in terms of discrete variables as follows:

$$q_{2t-1}^C - q_{2t-2}^C = (e_2 / \varepsilon)(\beta_{2t-1} - \beta_{2t-2}) \tag{5.4}$$

Substituting Equation 5.4 into Equation 5.2 and rearranging yields the following linear second-order difference equation for β_2 (the utility attrition rate for Good 2):

$$\beta_{2t} - \left\{ 1 - \beta_2 T(q_2^C)^2(e_2 / \varepsilon) \right\}\beta_{2t-1} - \beta_2 T /(q_2^C)^2(e_2 / \varepsilon)\beta_{2t-2} = 0 \tag{5.5}$$

The characteristic equation for Equation 5.5 is given by:

$$\lambda^2 - \left\{ 1 - \beta_2 T(q_2^C)^2(e_2 / \varepsilon) \right\}\lambda - \beta_2 T /(q_2^C)^2(e_2 / \varepsilon) = 0 \tag{5.6}$$

Equation 5.6 has distinct real roots $\lambda_1 = 1$ and $\lambda_2 = -\beta_2 T /(q_2^C)^2(e_2 / \varepsilon)$, which implies that the general solution of Equation 5.5 can be written as follows, where c_1 and c_2 are real constants:

$$\beta_2^t = c_1 + c_2 \left\{ -\beta_2 T /(q_2^C)^2(e_2 / \varepsilon) \right\}^t, \quad t = 1, 2, \cdots \tag{5.7}$$

When $t=0$: $\beta_2^0 = c_1 + c_2$
When $t=1$: $\beta_2^1 = c_1 - c_2 \left\{ \beta_2 T /(q_2^C)^2(e_2 / \varepsilon) \right\}$
When $t=2$: $\beta_2^2 = c_1 + c_2 \left\{ \beta_2 T /(q_2^C)^2(e_2 / \varepsilon) \right\}^2$
When $t=3$: $\beta_2^3 = c_1 - c_2 \left\{ \beta_2 T /(q_2^C)^2(e_2 / \varepsilon) \right\}^3$

It can be seen that β_2 (the utility attrition rate for Good 2) fluctuates cyclically around the real constant c_2. Note that the general solution does not diverge provided that $\beta_2 T /(q_2^C)^2(e_2 / \varepsilon) \leq 1$.

The above equations demonstrating the manner in which β_2 (the utility attrition rate for Good 2) fluctuates are based on the linear approximation $q_2^c = d_2 + e_2(\beta_2/\varepsilon)$. Substituting this into Equation 5.1 provides a rough indication of the manner in which the equilibrium level of household employment (T_L^*) fluctuates, while substituting into

Human Psychology and Economic Fluctuation

Equation 4.31 provides a rough indication of the manner in which the equilibrium levels of Good 1 and Good 2 (q_1^* and q_2^*) fluctuate.

1.2. Monetary Factors and Their Impact on the Economic Cycle

Until now we have considered the economic cycle in terms of "real" utility attrition based on linear or non-linear increasing-gradient utility attrition functions such as those shown in Figure 5.1 (a) and (b). However, as we discussed in Section 3 of Chapter 2, the generalized (relative) utility attrition rate depends not only on the utility attrition function, but also on changes in a household's expected utility from goods (E_1). If an upturn in the economy makes firms more willing to buy or rent assets owned by households, such that the monetary value of these assets increases, then that will serve to increase households' expected future income and thus their expected utility from goods (E_1), such that their generalized utility attrition rate will also increase. In other words, in addition to "real" factors that depend on the form of the utility attrition function, monetary factors—changes to the monetary value of household assets that are attributable to corporate behavior—can also have an impact on the economic cycle. We now discuss the mechanism by which this might occur.

The generalized (relative) utility attrition rate was defined as follows in Section 3 of Chapter 2:

$$\beta(t) = -\frac{dU(t)}{dt} + \frac{dE_1}{dt} \tag{5.8}$$

The first term on the right-hand side of Equation 5.8 represents "real" factors captured by the utility attrition function, while the second term represents "monetary" factors corresponding to changes in a household's expected utility from goods (E_1) over time. Changes in the generalized (relative) utility attrition rate are determined by changes in each of these terms.

The relationship between "real" factors (the first term on the right-hand side of Equation 5.8) and the economic cycle was discussed in the previous section: the "real" utility attrition rate fluctuates in a cyclical fashion that is driven by the existence of a non-linear increasing-gradient utility attrition function. The remainder of this section focuses on changes to the second term on the right-hand side of Equation 5.8, which may be attributed to changes in corporate behavior as they relate to the level of demand for assets owned by households. This process may be summarized as follows:

(1) Increase in the real utility attrition rate during an economic upswing
→(2) increase in household demand for consumer goods
→(3) increase in corporate profits
→(4) increase in lending (active investment) by the banking system to firms
→(5) increase in firms' demand for land, buildings, and other household assets
→(6) increase in the monetary value of household assets
→(7) increase in households' expected future income
→(8) increase in households' expected utility from goods (E_1).

(1) corresponds to an increase in the first term on the right-hand side of Equation 5.8, while (8) corresponds to an increase in the second term. Changes in the second term (and their size) depend directly on corporate behavior, but also depend indirectly on changes in the first term (and their size). As such, we would argue that changes in the second term are likely to lag behind changes in the first term in a cyclical fashion. Figure 5.3 presents a sketch of this mechanism, with the dotted line (i) depicting movements in the first term, while the dotted line (ii) depicts (lagging) changes in the second term. The solid line (iii) depicts the behavior of the generalized (relative) utility attrition rate, which is determined by summing (i) and (ii). Changes in the generalized (relative) utility attrition rate trigger changes in directly observable real variables via our "basic equation of labor" and the demand functions for each good.

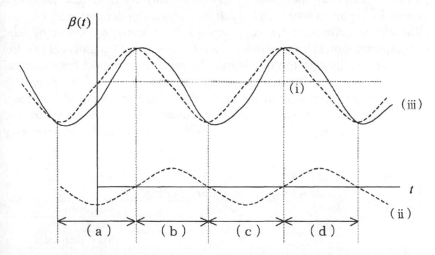

Figure 5.3 Behavior of the generalized (relative) utility attrition rate, which is determined by summing movements in the first term and (lagging) changes in the second term of Equation 5.8

As can be seen from Figure 5.3, the solid curve (iii) depicting changes in the generalized utility attrition rate (taking monetary factors into account) lies to the right of the dotted curve (i), which depicts changes in the real utility attrition rate (corresponding to changes in the first term on the right-hand side of Equation 5.8). In the remainder of this section we use Figure 5.3 to discuss the mechanism by which the economic cycle may be affected by monetary factors.

The real utility attrition rate $-dU/dt$ (human desire) is in an upward phase of its cycle throughout interval (a) in Figure 5.3, but dE_1/dt does not begin to increase until midway through the period, such that the increase in the generalized utility attrition rate $\beta(t)$ lags slightly behind the increase in the real utility attrition rate $(-dU/dt)$. Furthermore, the pace of increase in the generalized utility attrition rate peaks during the second half of interval (a), and then gradually declines. Moving ahead to the next period, the real utility attrition rate is in a downward phase of its cycle throughout interval (b), but dE_1/dt does not begin to decrease until midway through the period, such that the decrease in the generalized utility attrition rate $\beta(t)$ lags slightly behind the decrease in the real utility attrition rate $(-dU/dt)$. Furthermore, the pace of decrease in the generalized utility attrition rate peaks during the second half of interval (a), and then gradually declines. Interval (c) is a cyclical repetition of interval (a), while interval (d) is a cyclical repetition of interval (b).

In Figure 5.3, monetary factors create a time lag between changes in human demand psychology and changes in the real economy by (partially) offsetting increases in the real utility attrition rate when the economy is in an upswing and (partially) offsetting decreases in the real utility attrition rate when the economy is in a downswing. As can be seen by comparing dotted curve (i) with solid curve (iii) over interval (a), the generalized utility attrition rate is initially receiving support from the real utility attrition rate alone, but in the second half of the interval is receiving support from both the real utility attrition rate and monetary factors. As such, we can break the economic cycle down into four different phases depending on the contributions of real and monetary factors:

Phase	$-dU/dt$ (real factors)	dE_1/dt (monetary factors)	$\beta(t)$
Phase 1	Rising	Falling	Falls, then rises
Phase 2	Rising	Rising	Rising
Phase 3	Falling	Rising	Rises, then falls
Phase 4	Falling	Falling	Falling

Table 5.2 Stages of the economic cycle, taking monetary factors into account

1.3. The Formation and Collapse of a Financial Bubble

The changes in expected utility from goods ("monetary factors") considered in the previous section arise as a secondary consequence of endogenous changes in the real utility attrition rate. As such, one would not expect to see the economic cycle being driven by monetary factors in most cases.

However, history has demonstrated that monetary factors may sometimes take over as the driving force behind the economic cycle, resulting in the formation (and eventual collapse) of a financial bubble. This occurs when the increase in dE_1/dt is excessively large during Phase 2 (see previous table) as a result of the combined effects of credit provided by the banking system (or by one firm to another) and an increase in the monetary value of assets that have been purchased for speculative or pure investment purposes, such that the economy maintains its upward momentum in Phase 3 (due to excessive investment or speculation) despite a decline in the real utility attrition rate (the level of human desire).

On the demand side, an increase in households' expected future income—due to the impact of monetary factors—makes it easier for households to purchase goods that would be unaffordable (and are therefore beyond the scope of desire) at "usual" income levels (primarily luxury goods). A bubble economy is initially driven by this increase in desire, and is then supported by consumption externalities. On the production side, firms either respond to household demand by expanding their production of existing luxury goods via pure investment, or seek to stimulate demand by launching new luxury goods onto the market. Households maintain high levels of consumer spending, and firms maintain high levels of production and profits, such that everybody is happy with the booming economy.

However, a bubble economy of this nature is driven by *monetary* utility attrition resulting from the increased affordability of existing products (and the corresponding increase in human desire for goods), and eventually—as a result of excessive bank credit or other supporting factors—reaches the point where monetary utility attrition is completely out of balance with *real* utility attrition, which is driven by pure investment activity (on the part of firms) aimed at creating new products or new functionality. Once households and firms realize this and begin to have doubts regarding the economic outlook, and once consumers begin to tire of purchasing luxury products for which they have little if any real desire, then households are likely to reduce their spending on consumption goods, and firms are likely to scale back their production. Once the economy begins to turn downwards, the desire of firms to purchase or rent household assets (particularly real assets such as land and buildings) for pure investment purposes will diminish, causing the monetary value of these assets to fall sharply. Furthermore, once households' expected utility from goods (E_1) stops rising, the generalized (relative) utility attrition rate will immediately fall back to the level of the real utility attrition rate. This adjustment process represents the collapse of a financial bubble, with the economy shifting rapidly from Phase 3 to Phase 4 (see Figure 5.4) as previous overshooting (due to monetary factors) is corrected.

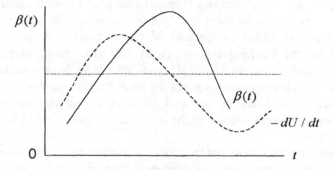

Figure 5.4 Collapse of a financial bubble (an immediate adjustment process of the generalized (relative) utility attrition rate to the level of the real utility attrition rate)

Even when the economy moves back into Phase 1 and the real utility attrition rate $-dU/dt$ begins to rise once again, the generalized utility attrition rate may continue to fall due to an ongoing (sharp) decline in the second term on the right-hand side of Equation 5.8 as a result of negative wealth effects (stemming from a decline in the monetary value of household assets) or households' expectations that the nation's worsening fiscal position will result in increased taxes and other financial burdens at some point in the future.

Furthermore, a bubble economy causes a society's production capital to be shifted into the production of those luxury goods for which demand has increased, such that excessive investment occurs in these sectors. Once the bubble collapses and monetary factors begin to have a negative impact, the decline in expected utility from luxury goods will be larger than the decline in expected utility from necessities. This means that households' demand for luxury goods—having grown excessive due to the impact of monetary factors—will fall away sharply, thereby reducing the profitability of production capital that has been shifted into production of luxury goods and causing corporate earnings to deteriorate sharply. The economy may also come under pressure on the financial front if banks begin to face difficulties in recovering funds owed by firms and decide to reduce the proportion of their funds that is "actively" invested (in loans to firms), thereby causing the money multiplier to fall. Once the bubble bursts, expected utility from goods will fall in a reversal of the process described in the previous section ((1)–(8)), and this chain of events will serve to accelerate the economy's decline.

As a result of an increase in the monetary utility attrition rate, a bubble economy causes social capital and labor to be allocated in a manner that does not properly reflect the actual desire of consumers (households). The bigger the bubble, the greater the problems that may be left behind in its wake. Furthermore, if households have updated their stock of consumption goods—such that they own all the latest goods—by the time that the bubble bursts, then even if the government seeks to stimulate the post-bubble economy via fiscal and/or monetary policy measures aimed at boosting households' purchasing power, it is likely that households will use any additional funds to increase their savings or pay off existing debt rather than using these funds to buy new consumption goods. As such, the government is likely to enjoy little success in its efforts to stimulate the economy until households' stock of consumption goods grows old or outdated.

It should be clear from the above discussion that it is much more difficult for an economy to recover from a bubble than from a "normal" cyclical recession. As such, government officials and other key policy-makers should keep a particularly close eye on developments relating to real factors and monetary factors whenever the economy is in the latter stages of an upward phase, and should take appropriate action whenever any signs of bubble-like psychology (as embodied in monetary factors) are detected.

1.4. Changes in Industrial Structure and Their Impact on the Economic Cycle

As we discussed in the first section of this chapter, the fundamental drivers of the endogenous economic cycle are: (a) the existence of goods with non-linear increasing-gradient utility attrition functions (increasing utility attrition rates); and (b) the inverse relationship between the level of household employment (or output levels) and the utility attrition rate (the fundamental driver of demand). As such, any change in industrial structure that alters the relative market shares of goods with linear utility attrition functions and goods with non-linear increasing-gradient utility attrition functions can be expected to have an impact on the economic cycle. Specifically, if the overall proportion of goods with linear utility attrition functions increases as a result of increased demand for such goods, then the portion of the economic cycle that is determined by real factors will have a smaller amplitude, such that peaks will be lower and troughs will be shallower. Conversely, if the overall proportion of goods with non-linear increasing-gradient utility attrition functions increases as a result of increased demand for such goods, then the portion of the economic cycle that is determined by real factors will have a greater amplitude, such that peaks will be higher and troughs will be deeper.

Ever since the industrial revolution, the industrial structures of developed nations have increasingly centered around secondary (manufacturing) industries, such that durable consumer items and other goods with non-linear increasing-gradient utility attrition functions have expanded their market share. This gradual change in industrial structure has played a major role in the emergence of endogenous economic cycles.

More recently, however, the ratio of tertiary (service) industries to secondary (manufacturing) industries has been increasing in developed nations. It can be argued that services have linear utility attrition functions (as do expendable supplies, clothing, and foodstuffs), and that this increase in the overall proportion of goods and services with linear utility attrition functions will (in developed nations) serve to reduce the amplitude of that portion of the economic cycle that is determined by real factors. This point is perhaps worthy of discussion at a later time.

2. Human Psychology and Economic Growth

In this section we remove the assumption that pure investment undertaken by firms during a given period of time has no impact on utility attrition rates or labor productivity parameters for the same period, and consider the relationship between economic growth (as described by our "basic equation of labor") and changes in parameters (utility attrition rates and labor productivity parameters) resulting from pure investment by firms.

2.1. Pure Investment Activity by Firms and Economic Growth

As we discussed in Section 2.3 of Chapter 1, firms undertake pure investment that is financed by (the entire amount of) household savings, raising funds either directly (by issuing shares and/or bonds) or indirectly (via the banking system). This pure investment activity enables firms to provide new types of consumption goods or add new features or functionality to existing consumption goods. By providing households with a broader range of options, this investment activity serves to increase the household sector's total level of desire for consumption goods, such that its utility attrition rates would also increase.

For example, if a firm launches a consumption good (Good *h*) that is completely new to households (consumers), then the firm will face the fixed costs associated with the development of a new production technology ($q_h = b_h T_{Lh}^{1-a}$) as well as wages and other variable costs that must be incurred in order to produce initial inventory. If Good *h* proves attractive to consumers once it is made available, then households will be willing to purchase that good by running down their savings, borrowing from the banking system, or diverting funds with which they had been planning to purchase other consumption goods. This will increase their expected utility from Good *h* (E_{1h}), resulting in a new generalized (relative) utility attrition rate (β_h) due to the impact on the second term on the right-hand side of Equation 5.8. Once Good *h* captures a certain share of the total market for consumption goods and develops a loyal customer base, the expected utility from goods (E_1) will stop rising, and the utility attrition rate will depend on the first term on the right-hand side of Equation 5.8 (which derives from the actual utility attrition function). In other words, if a new consumption good is sufficiently attractive to become the object of human desire, then it will generate ongoing demand from households, enabling firms to recoup their initial costs and earn profits on top of these costs.

If households are willing to support a firm in its plans to launch a new consumption good (Good *h*), then a production function $q_h(T_{Lh})$ (production capital) will be maintained on an ongoing basis, and Good *h* will have a positive utility attrition rate (β_h), such that the relationship between the new utility attrition rate and the new productivity parameter for Good *h* can be written as β_h/b_h. Equation 4.28 (our "basic equation of labor") can be augmented as follows to include this ratio:

$$T_L^* = \frac{(\beta_1/b_1)^{2/3} + (\beta_2/b_2)^{2/3} + (\beta_h/b_h)^{2/3}}{(\beta_1/b_1)^{2/3} + (\beta_2/b_2)^{2/3} + (\beta_h/b_h)^{2/3} + (a\varepsilon)^{2/3}}(T-l) \qquad (5.9)$$

If we assume that the new consumption good (Good *h*) is not a substitute for either of the existing consumption goods (Goods 1 and 2), then the emergence of Good *h* will have no impact on β_1/b_1 or β_2/b_2, and the inclusion of β_h/b_h in both the numerator and the denominator of our "basic equation of labor" will cause the equilibrium employment level T_L^* to increase from its previous level.

However, if the new consumption good is a substitute for one of the existing consumption goods, then the emergence of Good *h* will reduce a consumer's expected utility from that good, thereby reducing the generalized (relative) utility attrition rate for that good due to the impact on the second term on the right-hand side of Equation 5.8. As such, the ratio of the utility attrition rate to the productivity parameter for that good (β_1/b_1 or β_2/b_2, depending on which of the existing goods is affected by the emergence of a substitute) will decline, thereby (partially) offsetting the increase in the equilibrium employment level T_L^* that results from the launch of the new consumption good.

Despite this, however, we would expect ongoing pure investment—which enables firms to provide new types of consumption goods or add new features or functionality to existing consumption goods—to bring about ongoing increases in the equilibrium employment level T_L^* as described by our "basic equation of labor". As a result of this process, goods with low labor productivity (low price competitiveness) will gradually be eliminated, such that the economy's (society's) overall level of labor productivity (technology) will gradually improve. This will enable the society to achieve ongoing economic growth (defined as sustained increases in the total level of output). If the number of households remains constant, then the number of hours worked by each household (in equilibrium) will increase as a result of economic growth. However, income per household will also increase, providing each household with a greater economic capacity to raise children, such that new households (population growth) would likely be created as a result of decisions made (autonomously) by households. As such, income per household and equilibrium work hours (employment) against a backdrop of economic growth are determined by the balance between the increase in actual output levels and the increase in the number of households (population).

The above analysis implies that if pure investment activity stalls and an "old" equilibrium (based on "old" consumption goods or products with outdated features) continues for an extended period of time, then the range of goods for which households feel a positive utility attrition rate (desire) will gradually shrink, and utility attrition rates for the existing consumption goods will also decline as households grow tired of consuming them. As such, the equilibrium employment level T_L^* will fall, and economic activity will stall.

2.2. A Brief Consideration of Technological Innovation

In Section 3 of Chapter 2, we argued that firms must undertake pure investment—aimed at launching new products, adding new functionality to existing products, or boosting households' real income by lowering supply prices—in order to expand the range of goods for which households feel a positive utility attrition rate as well as boosting utility attrition rates for existing goods. This argument shares certain similarities with J. A. Schumpeter's theory of innovation (defined as "new combinations of existing stock of the factors of production"). Our theory of economic growth (outlined in the previous section) is also essentially the same as Schumpeter's argument that the essence of capitalism (and technological progress) lies in continuing changes to the form of the production function. As such, our generalized "basic equation of labor" (for the case of many goods) can perhaps be viewed as a formalization of innovation theory, with old equilibria constantly being undermined by the sudden emergence of new innovations and replaced by new equilibria based on new products and new production technologies. These new products and new production technologies cause consumers to experience a positive utility attrition rate (a positive level of desire), thereby providing demand-side support for those firms that have invested in innovations.

NOTES

1. Here we assume that for any given good, the proportion of households with non-linear decreasing-gradient utility attrition functions is very small by comparison with the proportion of households with linear utility attrition functions or non-linear increasing-gradient utility attrition functions, where "gradient" refers to the absolute value of the curve slope at any given point. This makes it possible to use either a linear utility attrition function or a non-linear increasing-gradient utility attrition function once the households are aggregated.
2. From Equations 4.28 and 4.31, the relationship between the equilibrium level of (household) employment and the equilibrium output levels of Good 1 and Good 2 can be expressed as follows:

$$q_1^* = \left\{ \frac{(\beta_1/b_1)^{2/3}}{(\beta_1/b_1)^{2/3}+(\beta_2/b_2)^{2/3}} \right\}^{1/2} b_1(T_L^*)^{1/2}$$

$$q_2^* = \left\{ \frac{(\beta_2/b_2)^{2/3}}{(\beta_1/b_1)^{2/3}+(\beta_2/b_2)^{2/3}} \right\}^{1/2} b_2(T_L^*)^{1/2}$$

Chapter 6

The Effectiveness of Aggregate Demand Management Policy

In this chapter we use the "loanable funds theory" of classical macro-economic theory (discussed in Section 2.1 of Chapter 4) to analyze the mechanism by which aggregate demand management policy (monetary and fiscal policy) can alter households' monetary utility attrition rates and thereby have an impact on various economic variables, and then show that it is possible to construct a model in which changes to utility attrition rates cause the money market and real markets to interact. In order to simplify our analysis, we omit any discussion of cash hoarding by households and firms or "induced investment" that depends on income or production.

1. Controllable Loan Balances and Utility Attrition

1.1. The Relationship Between Market Interest Rates and Utility Attrition

We begin by showing that changes to market interest rates can alter households' monetary utility attrition rates due to the impact that such changes have on households' "controllable loan balances". A household's "controllable loan balance" is the amount of debt that it is able to service without facing any undue financial burden: an increase in a household's controllable loan balance represents an increase in its buying power, while a decrease in a household's controllable loan balance represents a reduced capacity to purchase goods.

If we denote a household's controllable loan balance by L_c, the market interest rate by r_m, and the average repayment period by n, then the household's loan repayment amount (B_c), where it repays loan interest and principal in equal installments, can be expressed as:

$$B_C = \frac{r_m(1+r_m)^n}{(1+r_m)^n - 1} L_C \tag{6.1}$$

We may also write $B_C = \overline{U_W}$, where $\overline{U_W}$ denotes the (constant) amount of household savings that can be allocated to loan repayments. Substituting $B_C = \overline{U_W}$ into Equation 6.1 and rearranging yields the following expression for the household's controllable loan balance:

$$L_C = \frac{(1+r_m)^n - 1}{r_m(1+r_m)^n} \overline{U_W} \tag{6.2}$$

A household's controllable loan balance—as defined by Equation 6.2—represents the total amount that the household is able to borrow during the current period, that is, the total amount of buying power that it is able to access via borrowing.

If we assume that the average repayment period (n) is given, then a household's controllable loan balance (L_C) is determined by the market interest rate (r_m): as can be seen from Equation 6.2, a household's controllable loan balance falls when the market interest rate rises, and rises when the market interest rate falls. An increase (decrease) in a household's controllable loan balance represents an increase (decrease) in buying power, which affects the household's monetary utility attrition rate and thereby causes its expected utility from goods—the second term on the right-hand side of Equation 5.8—to increase (decrease). As such, an increase in the market interest rate (r_m) causes a household's generalized (relative) utility attrition rate to decline, while a decline in the market interest rate (r_m) causes a household's generalized (relative) utility attrition rate to increase. This relationship is illustrated by curve DE (where "DE" stands for "desire") in Figure 6.1. Note that β_1/ε denotes the household's generalized (relative) utility attrition rate for the reference good, $\overline{\beta_1/\varepsilon}$ denotes real utility attrition, $R_1(\overline{G})$ denotes monetary utility attrition stemming from a change in buying power as a result of the government's fiscal policy (that is, a transfer of future income to the present via issuance of government bonds; see Section 2.1 of this chapter), and $R_1(r_m)$ denotes monetary utility attrition stemming from the impact of the market interest rate (r_m) on the household's controllable loan balance.

Curve DE illustrates the behavior of households with respect to borrowing. In simple terms, households are more willing to take out loans in order to purchase consumption goods when market interest rates are low (implying that loan repayments are small), such that aggregate demand increases as interest rates fall. Similarly, households are less willing to take out loans when market interest rates are high (implying that loan repayments are large), such that aggregate demand decreases as interest rates rise.[1]

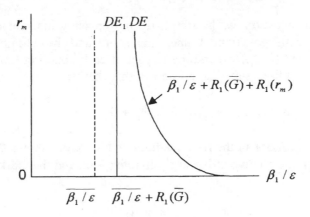

Figure 6.1 Relationship between the market interest rate and the household's generalized (relative) utility attrition rate

Note that the curve DE becomes a vertical line (DE_1) with equation $\beta_1/\varepsilon = \overline{\beta_1/\varepsilon} + R_1(\overline{G})$ if we ignore the impact of the market interest rate on monetary utility attrition (via changes to the household's controllable loan balance).

1.2. Equilibrium Conditions for the Loan Market

As we discussed in Section 2.1 of Chapter 4, if we consider currency creation by the banking system (ΔM) as a supply-side factor in the loan market and the net increase in the currency holdings of households and firms (ΔL) as a demand-side factor in the loan market, currency creation by the banking system can be expressed in volume terms as $\Delta M/p_3$ (that is, by dividing it by the price of the pure investment good), and adding this term to Equation 4.38 (the supply of pure investment goods) gives an expression for the supply of loanable funds in volume terms. This can be expressed in monetary terms as $S_W(\beta_1/\varepsilon,\overline{a})+\Delta\overline{M}$. Similarly, the net increase in the currency holdings of households and firms (ΔL) can be expressed in volume terms as $\Delta L/p_3$ (that is, by dividing it by the price of the pure investment good), and adding this term to Equation 4.41 (demand for pure investment goods) gives an expression for demand for loanable funds in volume terms. This can be expressed in monetary terms as $I_{P1}(\beta_1/\varepsilon)+I_{P2}(r_m)+\overline{I_D}+\Delta\overline{L}$. Equating supply and demand gives the equilibrium condition for the loan market in monetary terms:

$$S_W(\beta_1/\varepsilon,\bar{a}) + \triangle\overline{M} = I_{P1}(\beta_1/\varepsilon) + I_{P2}(r_m) + \overline{I}_D + \triangle\overline{L} \qquad (6.3)$$

This equation can be simplified by replacing independent investment ($\overline{I}_D$) with government spending ($\overline{G}$), and by eliminating induced investment ($I_{P1}(\beta_1/\varepsilon)$) and the impact of cash hoarding ($\triangle\overline{L}$) in line with the assumptions stated at the start of this chapter:

$$S_W(\beta_1/\varepsilon,\bar{a}) + \triangle\overline{M} = I_P(r_m) + \overline{G} \qquad (6.4)$$

Curve *ILSM* in the first quadrant of Figure 6.2 shows the relationship between the relative utility attrition rate (β_1/ε) and the market interest rate (r_m).

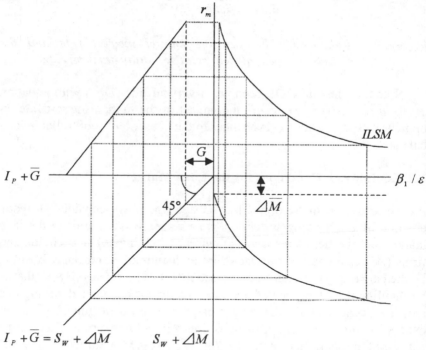

Figure 6.2 Relationship between the generalized (relative) utility attrition rate and the market interest rate based on the equilibrium conditions for the loan market

The relationship between the market interest rate (r_m) and demand for loans ($I_P + \overline{G}$) is shown in the second quadrant, the relationship between the relative utility attrition rate (β_1/ε) and the supply of loans $(S_w+\overline{\Delta M})$ is shown in the fourth quadrant, and the condition that supply equals demand is shown in the third quadrant.

1.3. Determination of the Utility Attrition Rate and the Market Interest Rate

Figure 6.3 combines Figure 6.1 and the first quadrant of Figure 6.2. If we ignore the impact of the market interest rate on monetary utility attrition (via changes to the household's controllable loan balance), then the market interest rate (r_m) is determined by the intersection of vertical line DE_1 with curve $ILSM$ at point e'. We use $r_m^{*'}$ to denote this level of the market interest rate. Under this scenario, we assume that the various factors in the loan market that affect curve $ILSM$ have no impact on households' utility attrition rates, in which case real variables such as the equilibrium levels of output and employment are not affected. However, if we take the impact of the market interest rate on monetary utility attrition (via changes to the household's controllable loan balance) into account, then the market interest rate (r_m) is determined by the intersection of curve DE with curve $ILSM$ at point e. We use r_m^{*} to denote this level of the market interest rate. Under this scenario, curve DE is downward-sloping to the right, such that the various factors in the loan market that affect curve $ILSM$ have an impact on households' monetary utility attrition rates and thus on their generalized (relative) utility attrition rates. This implies that factors in the loan market have an impact on real variables such as the equilibrium levels of output and employment.

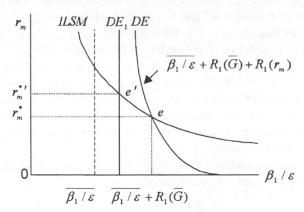

Figure 6.3 Determination of the market interest rate and the generalized (relative) utility attrition rate

We now explain the adjustment process by which a new intersection point (e) is reached following a shift in curve *ILSM* due to changes in loan market conditions.

The initial combination of the relative utility attrition rate (β_1/ε) and the market interest rate (r_m) is denoted in Figure 6.4 by point e, the intersection of curve *DE* and curve *ILSM*. Let us now assume that curve *ILSM* shifts downwards and to the left (to *ILSM'*) due to a change in loan market conditions (such as an increase in currency creation by the banking system ΔM). This causes the market interest rate to fall to r_m^1 (determined by the intersection of *ILSM'*—the equilibrium condition for the loan market—with the vertical line through e), which in turn causes the household's controllable loan balance (desire to purchase consumption goods using borrowed funds) to increase, such that the household's generalized (relative) utility attrition rate increases to the level consistent with point a on curve *DE*. This increase in the utility attrition rate then causes the market interest rate to fall (further) to r_m^2 (determined by the intersection of *ILSM'*—the equilibrium condition for the loan market—with the vertical line through a) due to an increase in household savings that increases the supply of funds in the loan market. This then brings about a further increase in the household's generalized (relative) utility attrition rate to the level consistent with point a' on curve *DE*. This process—a decline in the market interest rate, followed by an increase in the generalized (relative) utility attrition rate (an increase in aggregate demand), followed by an increase in household savings and hence the supply of loanable funds, which causes the market interest rate to decline further—is then repeated until the combination of the relative utility attrition rate (β_1/ε) and the market interest rate (r_m) reaches point e' (the intersection of curve *DE* with curve *ILSM'*).

Similarly, if curve *ILSM* shifts upwards and to the right, then the new intersection (of curve *DE* with curve *ILSM'*) is reached via the following process: an increase in the market interest rate is followed by a decrease in the generalized (relative) utility attrition rate (a decline in aggregate demand), which is then followed by a decrease in household savings and hence the supply of loanable funds, which causes the market interest rate to rise further (and so on).

A similar adjustment process occurs in cases where curve *DE* shifts and curve *ILSM* remains unchanged.

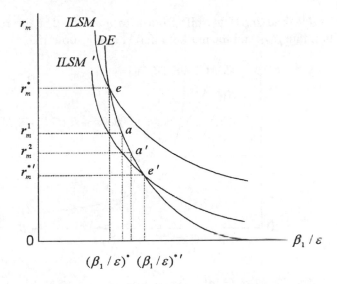

Figure 6.4 Adjustment process by which a new intersection point is reached following a shift in curve ILSM due to changes in loan market conditions

2. The Effectiveness of Aggregate Demand Management Policy and Characteristics of Our Theoretical Framework

2.1. The Effects of Fiscal Policy Action

We now extend the previous section's analysis to consider the impact of fiscal policy on the real economy. Suppose that the government adopts a fiscal policy of issuing an amount of government bonds that exceeds the prevailing level of bond redemptions, such that future income is transferred to the present and the level of economic activity is boosted via an increase in present-day buying power (aggregate demand).

An increase in government spending ($\overline{G}$) as a result of such a stance will cause the curve in the second quadrant of Figure 6.2 to shift to the left while maintaining its shape, such that curve *ILSM* in the first quadrant of Figure 6.2 will shift upwards and to the right. This transfer of future income to the present provides a direct boost to the purchasing power of households, such that the generalized (relative) utility attrition rate increases as a result of an increase in households' expected utility from goods (E_1) and curve *DE* shifts to the right while maintaining its shape as a result of the increase in $R_1(\overline{G})$. As can be seen from Figure 6.5, the increase in government spending ($\overline{G}$) causes the intersection of curves *DE* and *ILSM* to shift from *e* to *e'*, such that the relative utility attrition rate β_1/ε and the market interest rate r_m both rise.

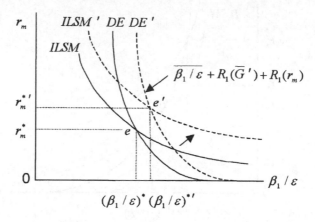

Figure 6.5 Effects of fiscal policy action

The above analysis demonstrates that an increase in the utility attrition rate as a result of increased fiscal spending serves to increase the equilibrium levels of employment and output via Equation 4.28 (our "basic equation of labor"). In other words, fiscal policy action has real (quantity) effects in our theoretical framework.

2.2. The Effects of Monetary Policy Action

We next consider the impact of monetary policy on the real economy. Suppose that the banking system (central bank) increases the money supply by an amount ΔM with a view to boosting the level of real economic activity.

An increase in the money supply will cause the curve in the fourth quadrant of Figure 6.2 to shift downwards while maintaining its shape, such that curve *ILSM* in the first quadrant of Figure 6.2 will shift downwards and to the left. As can be seen from Figure 6.6, this causes the intersection of curves *DE* and *ILSM* to shift from *e* to *e'*, such that the relative utility attrition rate β_1/ε rises and the market interest rate r_m falls.

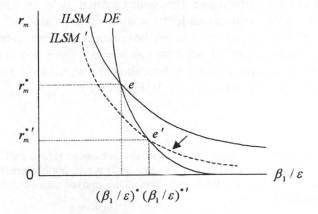

Figure 6.6 Effects of monetary policy action

The above analysis demonstrates that an increase in the utility attrition rate as a result of an increase to the money supply serves to increase the equilibrium levels of employment and output via Equation 4.28 (our "basic equation of labor"). In other words, monetary policy action has real (quantity) effects in our theoretical framework.

2.3. The Classical Dichotomy and Our Theoretical Framework

Having incorporated monetary elements into our model in Section 2 of Chapter 4, we have completed our theoretical framework by following the traditional approach of classical macroeconomic theory with regard to the mechanism by which the interest rate, price level, and money wage level are determined.

As is well known, classical macroeconomic theory is characterized by the so-called "classical dichotomy", whereby real variables such as the employment level, output levels, and real interest rates are determined via the labor market, macroeconomic production functions, and the goods market (and loan market), and changes in the quantity of money have no impact whatsoever on these real variables (as explained by the so-called "quantity theory of money"). According to classical macroeconomic theory, monetary policy affects price levels but has no impact on real variables, while fiscal policy alters the real interest rate in the goods market (and loan market), but has no impact on the employment level or output levels.

However, while it is possible to consider the classical dichotomy as a special case of our theoretical framework where the market interest rate and the generalized (relative) utility attrition rate are independent (that is, where we use the vertical line DE_1 with equation $\beta_1/\varepsilon = \overline{\beta_1/\varepsilon} + R_1(\overline{G})$ in Figure 6.1), it is also possible to analyze the impact of fiscal and monetary policy in cases where the market interest rate and the generalized (relative) utility attrition rate are correlated due to the impact of the market interest rate on a household's controllable loan balance (that is, where we use the curve DE in Figure 6.1).

NOTE

1. For example, if we assume that the average household repays its loan over ten years, a market interest rate of 5% (annualized) would imply a controllable loan balance approximately 25% higher than if the market interest rate were 10% (annualized).

Chapter 7

Dynamic Analysis of Demand Psychology and Policy Implications

In this chapter we analyze demand psychology based on a dynamic framework in which the representative household considers the amounts it is prepared to spend on "reconsumption" of goods ("purchase (decision) prices"), and look at economic stimulus measures that are likely to be highly effective from a short-term perspective. We then look at non-discriminatory spending policy that provides a boost to buying power for all households in accordance with the principle of fairness, and show that discriminatory (selective) policy targeting those specific households that are prepared to spend additional funds on consumption goods may be effective during a deep recession.

1. Derivation of the Purchase Price Function for a Representative Household

1.1. The Relationship Between Goods Supply Prices and a Household's Reconsumption Cycle

In this section we pave the way for an analysis of the representative household's demand psychology during the interval between purchases by using the demand functions for each good to derive the relationship between supply prices for each good and the household's reconsumption cycle.

Equation 4.6 shows the demand functions for each good in a monetary economy:

$$\left. \begin{array}{l} q_1 = \dfrac{(p_1\beta_1)^{1/2}}{(p_1\beta_1)^{1/2} + (p_2\beta_2)^{1/2}} \dfrac{I}{p_1} \\[3mm] q_2 = \dfrac{(p_2\beta_2)^{1/2}}{(p_1\beta_1)^{1/2} + (p_2\beta_2)^{1/2}} \dfrac{I}{p_2} \end{array} \right\} \qquad (4.6)$$

The reconsumption cycles for each good (τ_1, τ_2) are found by dividing T units of time by the amount of each good consumed within T units of time (q_1, q_2) in accordance with Equation 2.3:

$$\left.\begin{aligned}
\tau_1 &= \frac{T}{q_1} = \frac{(p_1\beta_1)^{1/2} + (p_2\beta_2)^{1/2}}{(p_1\beta_1)^{1/2}} \frac{p_1 T}{I} \\
\tau_2 &= \frac{T}{q_2} = \frac{(p_1\beta_1)^{1/2} + (p_2\beta_2)^{1/2}}{(p_2\beta_2)^{1/2}} \frac{p_2 T}{I}
\end{aligned}\right\}
\qquad (7.1)$$

In order to derive the relationship between the supply price of Good 1 and the representative household's reconsumption cycle, we rewrite the first equation in Equation 7.1 as follows:

$$\tau_1 = \left\{ p_1 + \left(\frac{p_2\beta_2}{\beta_1} \right)^{1/2} p_1^{1/2} \right\} \frac{T}{I}$$

Rearranging gives:

$$p_1 + \left(\frac{p_2\beta_2}{\beta_1} \right)^{1/2} p_1^{1/2} - \frac{I}{T}\tau_1 = 0 \qquad (7.2)$$

Equation 7.2 is a quadratic equation in $p_1^{1/2}$ that yields the following solution based on the requirement $(p_1^{1/2} > 0)$:

$$p_1^{1/2} = \frac{\left(\dfrac{p_2\beta_2}{\beta_1} + \dfrac{4I}{T}\tau_1 \right)^{1/2} - \left(\dfrac{p_2\beta_2}{\beta_1} \right)^{1/2}}{2} \qquad (7.3)$$

Squaring both sides of Equation 7.3 yields the relationship between the supply price of Good 1 and the representative household's reconsumption cycle for Good 1:

$$p_1 = \frac{2\left(\dfrac{p_2\beta_2}{\beta_1} \right) + \dfrac{4I}{T}\tau_1 - 2\left(\dfrac{p_2\beta_2}{\beta_1} \right)^{1/2}\left(\dfrac{p_2\beta_2}{\beta_1} + \dfrac{4I}{T}\tau_1 \right)^{1/2}}{4} \qquad (7.4)$$

This relationship is illustrated in Figure 7.1.

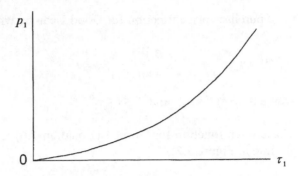

Figure 7.1 Relationship between the supply price of Good 1 and the optimal reconsumption cycle

The curve shown in Figure 7.1 is based on the first demand function in Equation 4.6, and describes the relationship between the supply price of Good 1 and the optimal reconsumption cycle under the assumption that other circumstances remain unchanged.

1.2. The Purchase Price Function for a Representative Household

In this section, we consider the representative household's willingness to spend on consumption goods at various points during the reconsumption cycle. Rather than assuming that the household is suddenly prepared to pay p_1^0 once each reconsumption cycle comes to an end ($t = \tau_1^0, 2\tau_1^0, ...$), we assume that the household is not prepared to pay anything immediately after making a purchase, but is willing to pay increasing amounts with the passage of time as a result of utility attrition (increasing desire), and eventually repurchases Good 1 when it is willing to pay p_1^0, the price at which Good 1 is being supplied.

We refer to the price that the representative household is willing to pay to repurchase Good i ($i=1,2$) as the "purchase decision price" or simply the "purchase price", which we denote by p_i^D, and refer to the function that describes the level of the purchase price at points during the reconsumption cycle as the "purchase price function", which we denote by $p_i^D(t)$.

If we assume that the purchase price for Good 1 increases at a constant rate over time (η_1), then this rate can be defined as the ratio of the supply price for Good 1 (p_1) to the reconsumption cycle for Good 1 (τ_1):

$$\eta_1 = \frac{p_1}{\tau_1} = \frac{p_1 q_1}{T} = \frac{(p_1 \beta_1)^{1/2}}{(p_1 \beta_1)^{1/2} + (p_2 \beta_2)^{1/2}} \frac{I}{T} \tag{7.5}$$

As such, the purchase price function for Good 1 can be written as:

$$p_1^D(t) = \eta_1 t = \frac{(p_1 \beta_1)^{1/2}}{(p_1 \beta_1)^{1/2} + (p_2 \beta_2)^{1/2}} \frac{I}{T} t \tag{7.6}$$

where $0 < p_1^D(t) < p_1^0$ and $0 < t < \tau_1^0$.

The purchase price function for Good 1 (Equation 7.6) is represented by the straight line in Figure 7.2.

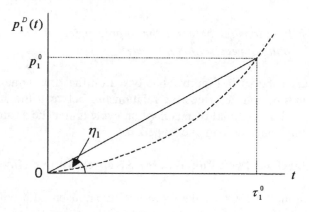

Figure 7.2 Purchase price function for Good 1 under the assumption that the purchase price for Good 1 increases at a constant rate over time (η_1)

It can be seen from Figure 7.2 that the representative household's purchase price is zero immediately after purchasing Good 1 at time $t=0$, but then increases steadily with the passage of time. Once a period of time equal to the reconsumption cycle has elapsed, the representative household's purchase price $p_1^D(t)$ is equal to the supply price p_1^0, and the household makes another purchase of Good 1.

Equation 7.5 shows that the rate at which the purchase price rises (η_1) increases when the supply price for Good 1 (p_1^0) rises, and decreases when the supply price for Good 1 falls.

Note that the above analysis applies identically to Good 2.

2. Derivation of the Cumulative Purchase Quantity Function and Dynamic Aspects of Demand

In this section we use the distribution of purchase prices across multiple households at any given point in time to derive the "cumulative purchase quantity function", which we then use to analyze demand for the household sector as a whole.

In order to simplify our analysis, we assume that Good 1 and Good 2 are (luxury) durable consumption goods with reconsumption cycles (τ_1, τ_2) that are longer than units of time T. We also assume that households have identical purchase price functions, and in order to ensure linearity of the cumulative purchase quantity function, we assume that consumption externalities across households can be ignored, and that the distribution of purchases across time is independent of the economic cycle (that is, we assume that the economic cycle does not cause purchases to be clustered or dispersed).

2.1. The Distribution of Purchase Prices Throughout the Household Sector and Derivation of the Cumulative Purchase Quantity Function

We now assume that there are N households in the economy (society). If we assume that these households behave independently from the perspective of consumption spending and that there are no consumption externalities across households, then the distribution of points in time at which goods are purchased should have an even spread. In order to simplify our analysis, we group the households into five equally-sized classes based on the timing of purchases, and in Figure 7.3 we draw the purchase price function for Good 1 $p_1^D(t)$ for each household that is on the boundary between classes, and show the distribution of purchase prices for these households at a given point in time ($t = \tau_1^0$).

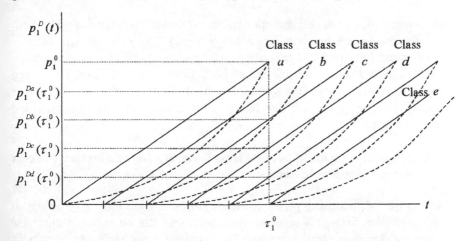

Figure 7.3 Distribution of purchase prices for the households that is on the boundary between classes at a given point in time ($t = \tau_1^0$)

Each of the classes (*a* through *e*) shown in Figure 7.3 consists of $N/5$ households. At time $t=\tau_1^0$, the households in Class *a* have purchase prices ranging between p_1^0 and $p_1^{Da}(\tau_1^0)$, the households in Class *b* have purchase prices ranging between $p_1^{Da}(\tau_1^0)$ and $p_1^{Db}(\tau_1^0)$, the households in Class *c* have purchase prices ranging between $p_1^{Db}(\tau_1^0)$ and $p_1^{Dc}(\tau_1^0)$, the households in Class *d* have purchase prices ranging between $p_1^{Dc}(\tau_1^0)$ and $p_1^{Dd}(\tau_1^0)$, and the households in Class *e* have purchase prices ranging between $p_1^{Dd}(\tau_1^0)$ and zero. Figure 7.4 shows the "cumulative purchase quantity function" based on the distribution of purchase prices at time $t=\tau_1^0$.

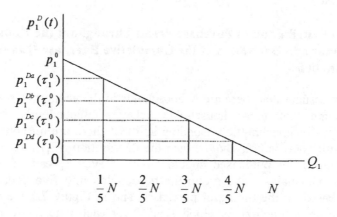

Figure 7.4　"Cumulative purchase quantity function" based on the distribution of purchase prices at time $t=\tau_1^0$

Figure 7.4 can be interpreted as follows. At time $t=\tau_1^0$, zero households have a purchase price that is higher than p_1^0, such that there is no demand for Good 1 at that price. All households have a purchase price that is higher than zero, such that all households demand Good 1 at a zero price. Similarly, two-fifths of all households have a demand price that is higher than $p_1^{Db}(\tau_1^0)$, such that two-fifths of all households demand Good 1 at that price.

2.2. Dynamic Aspects of the Demand Quantity Determination Process for the Household Sector

In Figure 7.4, purchase prices for households in each class (*a* through *e*) increase over time at a constant rate, such that the cumulative purchase quantity function shifts upwards (in parallel) over time, as shown in Figure 7.5.

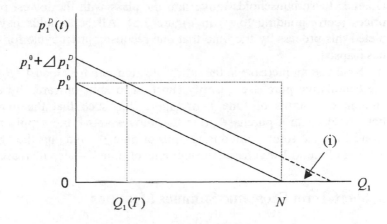

Figure 7.5 Cumulative purchase quantity function shifting upwards (in parallel) over time

The increase in the cumulative purchase quantity function (which we denote by Δp_1^D) is equal to the increase in purchase prices during units of time T. Substituting $t=T$ into the purchase price function $p_1^D(t)$ yields the following expression:

$$\Delta p_1^D = p_1^D(T) = \eta_1 T = \frac{(p_1\beta_1)^{1/2}}{(p_1\beta_1)^{1/2} + (p_2\beta_2)^{1/2}} I \tag{7.7}$$

Furthermore, as the slope of the cumulative purchase quantity function is equal to p_1/N, the number of households with a purchase price that moves above the supply price of Good 1 at some point during units of time T (that is, the number of households that decide to purchase Good 1 during units of time T) is given by $Q_1(T) = \Delta p_1^D \div p_1/N$, such that:

$$Q_1(T) = \frac{(p_1\beta_1)^{1/2}}{(p_1\beta_1)^{1/2} + (p_2\beta_2)^{1/2}} \frac{I}{p_1} N = q_1 N \tag{7.8}$$

Equation 7.8 states that the aggregate amount of Good 1 purchased during units of time T is equal to an individual household's demand for Good 1 (q_1, as given by Equation 4.6) multiplied by the number of households.

In Figure 7.5, $Q_1(T)$—the number of households with a purchase price that moves above the supply price of Good 1 (p_1^0) at some point during units of time T—represents the number of households that decide to purchase Good 1 during units of time T. Immediately after purchasing

Good 1, these households move into the class with the lowest purchase prices (corresponding to (i) in Figure 7.5). All households have completed this process by the time that one reconsumption cycle for Good 1 has elapsed.

Note that an increase in the utility attrition rate for Good 1 (β_1) causes the cumulative purchase quantity function to shift upwards by a larger amount over units of time T in Figure 7.5, such that the number of households with a purchase price that moves above the supply price of Good 1 (p_1^0) at some point during units of time T—and thus the aggregate amount of Good 1 purchased during units of time T—also increases.

3. Short-Term Economic Stimulus Measures

In this section we use our theoretical framework of utility attrition to examine economic stimulus measures that are likely to be highly effective from a short-term perspective.

3.1. The Impact of Non-Discriminatory Spending Policy

Action taken to stimulate a stalling economy typically takes the form of: (1) fiscal policy action (increased public works investment, tax cuts, etc. financed by an increase in government bond issuance); or (2) monetary policy action. For the purposes of our analysis, we consider such policy action to have the following impact on total household income.

(1) Fiscal policy: Transferal of future income to the present or a reduction in the tax levied on present income provides a direct boost for the total income of all households. In the case of increased public works investment, households working on public works projects are the first to benefit from such action.

(2) Monetary policy: A reduction in the market interest rate increases households' controllable loan balances, such that all households benefit from the higher total amount of buying power in real terms.

Such policies may be described as "non-discriminatory spending policies" in that the total income (buying power) of *all* households increases, and are attractive to policymakers in that they satisfy the "principle of fairness" with regard to public spending.

Let us now consider a non-discriminatory spending policy that increases aggregate demand by ΔG, such that the total income of all N households (considered as a whole) increases by ΔG. We assume that the entire amount of this increase in household income is used to purchase Good 1, a luxury durable consumer goods. Under this scenario, the income of each individual household increases by $\Delta G/N$, and each household's purchase price $p_1^D(t)$ increases by an equivalent amount, such that the cumulative purchase quantity function shifts upwards by $\Delta G/N$ as shown in Figure 7.6.

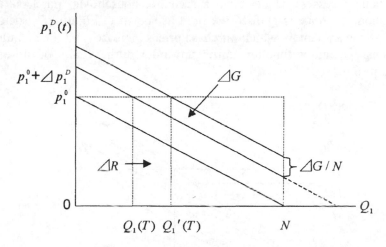

Figure 7.6 Impact of non-discriminatory spending policy

Those households corresponding to the interval between $Q_1(T)$ and $Q_1'(T)$ see their purchase price $p_1^D(t)$ rise above p_1^0 (the supply price for Good 1) as a result of this non-discriminatory spending policy, and therefore decide to purchase Good 1, such that sales (and consumption) of Good 1 increase by ΔR $[=p_1^0(Q_1'-Q_1)]$. All other households add the increase in income ($\Delta G/N$) to their savings. As such, the spillover effect on consumer spending is $\Delta R/\Delta G$ (>0), while the increase in household savings is $\Delta G-\Delta R$. The above analysis demonstrates that non-discriminatory spending policy is able to generate (short-term) demand during a time of recession.[1]

3.2. The Impact of Non-Discriminatory Spending Policy During a Deep Recession

We next consider the effectiveness of non-discriminatory spending policy during a post-bubble recession characterized by negative wealth effects (stemming from a decline in the monetary value of household assets) and/or households' expectations that the nation's worsening fiscal position will result in increased taxes and other financial burdens at some point in the future (a "deep recession").

As we discussed in Section 1.3 of Chapter 5, a deep post-bubble recession is such that even if the economy moves from Phase 4 into Phase 1 and the real utility attrition rate $-dU/dt$ begins to rise, the generalized utility attrition rate $\beta(t)$ (as defined by Equation 5.8) continues to fall due to the offsetting impact of monetary factors dE_1/dt (a correction of previous excesses). Under such a scenario, households' purchase price functions continue to shift to the right as shown in Figure 7.7, such that Δp_1^D—the amount by which purchase prices increase (and the cumulative purchase quantity function shifts upwards) during units of time T—declines.

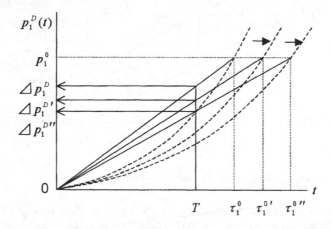

Figure 7.7 Successive decline of the amount by which purchase prices increase during T units of time under a "deep recession"

The effectiveness of non-discriminatory spending policy is likely to be severely reduced during a deep recession characterized by an ongoing decline in the (generalized) utility attrition rate $\beta(t)$. This is because the decline in the amount by which the cumulative purchase quantity function shifts upwards during units of time T offsets the impact of increased government spending in boosting the purchase prices of individual households, as shown in Figure 7.8.

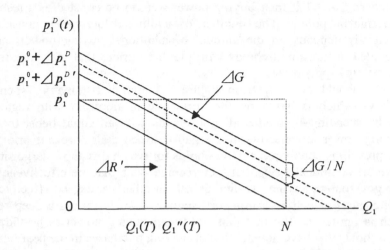

Figure 7.8 Reduced impact of non-discriminatory spending policy under a "deep recession"

The interval corresponding to households that see their purchase price $p_1^D(t)$ rise above p_1^0 (the supply price for Good 1) as a result of this non-discriminatory spending policy shrinks (by comparison with Figure 7.6) to the interval between $Q_1(T)$ and $Q_1''(T)$, such that the increase in sales (and consumption) of Good 1 $\Delta R'[=p_1^0(Q_1''-Q_1)]$ is smaller, as is the spillover effect on consumer spending $\Delta R'/\Delta G$. All other households—that is, the vast majority of households—add the increase in income ($\Delta G/N$) to their savings (thereby financing the increase in fiscal spending), such that there is very little impact on output or employment.

Furthermore, if households perceive the increase in government debt ΔD_G ($=\Delta G$) resulting from increased bond issuance as a threat to their future income, then the impact of non-discriminatory spending policy will be even further reduced as a result of a decline in expected utility from goods E_1 (that is, a decline in the generalized utility attrition rate).

3.3. Discriminatory Spending Policy and Its Effectiveness

Before considering economic stimulus measures that may prove effective even during a deep recession, it is first necessary to clarify the reasons why non-discriminatory spending policy is likely to have only limited success.

We begin by introducing the term "additional purchaser households" to describe those households with a purchase price $p_1^D(t)$ for Good 1 that is close to the supply price p_1^0, such that they could be expected to purchase Good 1 if their buying power were to be boosted as a result of government policy. The number of additional purchaser households obviously depends on the amount of additional buying power that is provided to those households with purchase prices that are close to the prevailing supply price.

As should be clear from Figure 7.8, non-discriminatory spending policy—which is based on the "principle of fairness" with regard to public spending—provides all households with an equal boost to their buying power, irrespective of the gap between their purchase price and the prevailing supply price. Households for which this gap is large simply save the additional funds that they receive, such that the effectiveness of the government's policy is diminished. In other words, the effectiveness (efficiency) of non-discriminatory spending policy during a deep recession is limited by the fact that additional buying power is provided to households that have no intention of making purchases in the near term.

With this in mind, we now consider a "discriminatory (or selective) spending policy" in which the number of additional purchaser households is increased by providing households with a greater boost to their buying power if their purchase price $p_1^D(t)$ for Good 1 is close to the supply price p_1^0, thereby resulting in a greater amount of consumer spending. Such a policy could be implemented by offering subsidies to those households that are prepared to purchase a given consumption good during a given period of time, with an estimate of the cumulative purchase quantity function for that particular good to be used in determining the necessary level of spending and the likely economic impact.

The cumulative purchase quantity function for Good 1 is shown in Figure 7.6. If the government were to offer a subsidy of Δg_1 to any household purchasing Good 1 during units of time T, then those households corresponding to the interval between $Q_1(T)$ and $Q_1''(T)$ in Figure 7.9 would be additional purchaser households (that is, households with a purchase price $p_1^D(t)$ greater than the subsidized supply price of $p_1^0 - \Delta g_1$).

The necessary amount of government spending $\Delta G'$ would depend on the cumulative purchase quantity function for Good 1 and would be equal to $\Delta g_1 Q_1''(T)$. Sales (and consumption) of Good 1 would increase by $\Delta R'$ $[=p_1^0(Q_1'' - Q_1)]$. Households corresponding to the interval between 0 and $Q_1(T)$ are those households that would have purchased Good 1 even without an incentive from the government, and so they would save the increase to its income (Δg_1). As such, the spillover effect on consumer spending is $\Delta R'/\Delta G'$ (>0), while the increase in household savings is $\Delta g_1 Q_1(T)$. The above analysis demonstrates that discriminatory spending policy is able to generate (short-term) demand during a time of deep recession.

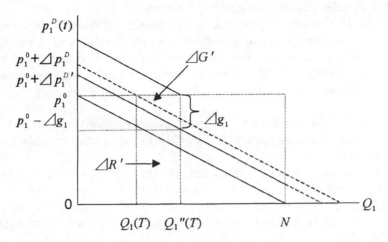

Figure 7.9 Impact of discriminatory spending policy under a "deep recession"

It should be clear that for the same level of government spending ($\Delta G = \Delta G'$), discriminatory spending policy creates a greater amount of (short-term) demand than non-discriminatory spending policy. This is because discriminatory spending policy does not involve any payment of funds to households with purchase prices $p_1^D(t)$ that are far below the supply price p_1^0 (that is, households corresponding to the interval between $Q_1'(T)$ and N in Figure 7.6), which means that other households can be provided with a greater boost to their buying power (thereby making them additional purchaser households). This reduces the amount of government spending that is "wasted" as household savings, and means that a greater number of households can be induced to make purchases.[2]

3.4. Estimating the Cumulative Purchase Quantity Function

We now consider the process of estimating the cumulative purchase quantity function, which could then be used to determine the necessary level of spending and the likely economic impact.

As we discussed in Section 2.1 of this chapter, the cumulative purchase quantity function describes the distribution of purchase prices across all households. It is therefore possible to count the number of households (or individuals in the case of goods purchased by individual consumers rather than households) with purchase prices at various levels between zero and the prevailing supply price, use a function to approximate the resulting distribution, and then use integration (beginning with households with higher purchase prices) to obtain an estimate of the cumulative purchase quantity function.

The distribution of purchase prices across all households could be estimated by conducting a survey of a random sample of households. Participants in such a survey could be asked to provide the following information (where Good 1 is the consumption good being considered by the government for subsidization):

1. Does the household have any desire (utility attrition) for Good 1?
   (If "yes", then the household would be asked to answer the following questions.)
2. Price levels at which the household is planning to (re)purchase Good 1.
3. Was Good 1 purchased during a given (previous) period of time?
4. The household's purchase price for Good 1 (the price that the household is currently prepared to pay to purchase or repurchase Good 1).

Let us now consider an example where n out of N households are surveyed regarding their willingness to purchase Good 1 at a price p_1^0, all n households are found to have a desire (utility attrition) for Good 1, and the distribution of purchase prices is found to follow the uniform distribution shown in Figure 7.10.

Those households that were found to have purchased Good 1 during the previous period would correspond to the interval between 0 and h.

The number of households

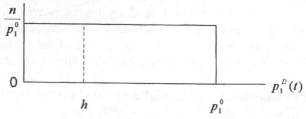

Figure 7.10 Sample distribution of purchase prices

Households with a purchase price of h purchased Good 1 at the start of the previous period, and we may therefore infer that purchase prices increase by h during the period in question (assuming that the previous period and the period in question are of equal lengths). In Figure 7.11, Z denotes the cumulative purchase quantity function at the start of units of time T (which is determined by integrating the above distribution function for purchase prices between p_1^0 and zero), while Z' denotes the cumulative purchase quantity function at the end of units of time T (which is determined by integrating the above distribution function for purchase prices between $p_1^0 + h$ and h).

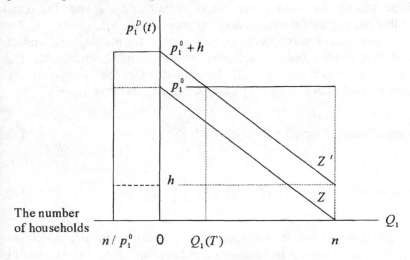

Figure 7.11 Cumulative purchase quantity function at the start and the end of units of time

The cumulative purchase quantity function for Good 1 at the start of units of time T is determined by using the distribution function and subtracting the number of households with purchase prices between zero and a given purchase price from the total number of households. Shifting this function upwards by h then gives the cumulative purchase quantity function for Good 1 at the end of units of time T. Q_1 can be expressed as follows:

$$Q_1 = n - \int_0^{p_1^D} \frac{n}{p_1^0} dp_1^D = n\left(1 - \frac{p_1^D}{p_1^0}\right)$$

Thus:

Start of units of time T: $p_1^D = p_1^0 - \left(\frac{p_1^0}{n}\right)Q_1$ (7.9)

End of units of time T: $p_1^D = (p_1^0 + h) - \left(\frac{p_1^0}{n}\right)Q_1$ (7.10)

The total amount purchased by the sampled households during units of time T, $Q_1(T)$, is equal to nh/p_1^0, which may be determined either by multiplying the height of the distribution function n/p_1^0 by the increase in purchase prices h, or by finding the intersection of the cumulative purchase quantity function at the end of units of time T with the horizontal line passing through the prevailing supply price p_1^0.

Once cumulative purchase quantity functions for the start and end of units of time T have been determined for the sampled households, the corresponding functions for *all* households can be estimated by multiplying each function by N/n along the horizontal axis.

$$\text{Start of units of time } T: \quad p_1^D = p_1^0 - \left(\frac{p_1^0}{N}\right)Q_1' \tag{7.11}$$

$$\text{End of units of time } T: \quad p_1^D = (p_1^0 + h) - \left(\frac{p_1^0}{N}\right)Q_1' \tag{7.12}$$

If the government is considering a non-discriminatory spending policy, then the resulting increases to consumer spending and household savings can be estimated by shifting the cumulative purchase quantity function for the end of units of time T upwards by $\Delta G/N$ (the amount of additional income per household). If the government is considering a discriminatory spending policy, then it can use the cumulative purchase quantity function for the end of units of time T to estimate the additional amounts of consumer spending and household savings that would result from a subsidy of Δg_1 (as well as the amount of government spending that such a subsidy would require).

3.5. Points to Consider Regarding Discriminatory Spending Policy

We conclude this chapter by considering three issues in relation to discriminatory spending policy (subsidies):

(1) Should a subsidy be a fixed amount, or a fixed proportion of the supply price?
(2) Should a subsidy be paid in cash (or by check), or should it take the form of a tax cut or a reduction of loan interest rates?
(3) Should a subsidy be accompanied by a (limited-time) tax on ownership of old consumption goods?

(1) Should a subsidy be a fixed amount, or a fixed proportion of the supply price?

In cases where the band of prices at which households intend to purchase the consumption good is narrow, a policy of paying a fixed-amount subsidy may be desirable due to its simplicity. However, where the band of prices is relatively wide, a fixed-amount subsidy will benefit a household purchasing a low-price good significantly more than it benefits a household purchasing a high-price good, thereby impinging on free choice and providing certain households with less incentive to buy. In such cases, it may be better to pay each household a subsidy that is equal to a fixed proportion of the price for which it purchases the consumption good in question.

(2) Should a subsidy be paid in cash (or by check), or should it take the form of a tax cut or a reduction of loan interest rates?

A subsidy paid in cash (or by check) or delivered in the form of a tax cut provides a quick boost to households' buying power, but may not result in increased tax revenue for quite some time. As such, it is necessary for the government to finance such a subsidy by issuing long-term bonds. However, a subsidy that is delivered in the form of a partial or full rebate of households' loan interest or hire-purchase interest payments throughout the relevant loan period can be paid in installments over time, such that it might not be necessary for the government to issue long-term bonds. Other possibilities to be considered: a cash subsidy could possibly be implemented by having households transfer their right to claim the subsidy to the company selling the product in exchange for a lower sale price; and in the case of interest subsidies, the lender might be able to offer loans or sales finance at lower interest rates in exchange for the right to claim the difference as a deduction from its corporation tax bill.

(3) Should a subsidy be accompanied by a (limited-time) tax on owner-ship of old consumption goods?

It is also possible to encourage households to purchase a new consumption good by levying a tax on households owning an old version of that consumption good for a limited period around the time that a subsidy is available.

The combination of a tax and a subsidy could prove more effective than a subsidy alone by providing households with both a reason to get rid of their existing version of the consumption good in question and a reason to purchase a new version of that consumption good. A tax on ownership of old consumption goods could also be used to finance a subsidy, in which case income would be transferred from households that continue to own old goods to households that replace old goods with new goods. Such an approach would be consistent with the intention of discriminatory spending policy by having allocations to households and impositions on households depend on the amount of risk borne by each household (that is, households bearing a greater risk would receive a larger boost to their buying power).

NOTES

1. Note that we have considered a one-off increase in government spending (where the increase in demand occurs just once during units of time T) rather than ongoing policy action. As such, we do not consider cumulative spillover effects on consumer spending and savings.
2. For example, in 1997 the Italian government sought to boost consumer spending by offering a subsidy to any household that replaced its existing car with a new car.

Chapter 8
A Summary of Our Theoretical Framework

This chapter concludes the book by summarizing the characteristics of our theory of utility attrition from the perspectives of macroeconomic and microeconomic theory, and presents some material that may help readers gain a better understanding of our framework. We also discuss some important issues—such as underemployment equilibrium analysis—that we have been unable to consider in sufficient detail in this book.

1. A Summary of Our Theoretical Framework and Its Characteristics

1.1. A Summary from the Perspective of Microeconomic Theory

The following is a summary—from a microeconomic perspective—of our theoretical framework for analysis of a monetary economy (developed in Chapter 4).

(Unknown variables)

$q_1, q_2, q_3^{IP}, w/p_1, p_2/p_1, p_3/p_1, P_1, P_2, P_3, I, T_L, r, p_1$ (13 in total)

q_1, q_2 denote the quantities of the consumption goods (Goods 1 and 2, which are also renewal investment goods), q_3^{IP} denotes the quantity of the pure investment good (Good 3, which is also a renewal investment good), w/p_1 denotes the real wage, p_2/p_1 and p_3/p_1 denote the prices of Goods 2 and 3 relative to the price of Good 1, P_1, P_2, P_3 denote the profits of each production division, I denotes total household income, T_L denotes labor time, r denotes the natural interest rate, and p_1 denotes the price level (the price of the reference good, Good 1).

(Parameters)

Households: $\beta_1, \beta_2, \varepsilon, a, T, l$
Firms: $b_1, b_2, b_3, \overline{q}_3, h, \mu, \rho, \overline{C}_1, \overline{C}_2$
Central bank: H
Commercial banks: re
Households and firms: cc

(Equations)

$$q_1 = \frac{1}{1+(p_2/p_1)^{1/2}(\beta_2/\beta_1)^{1/2}}\frac{I}{p_1} \qquad (A.1)$$

$$q_2 = \frac{(p_2/p_1)^{1/2}(\beta_2/\beta_1)^{1/2}}{1+(p_2/p_1)^{1/2}(\beta_2/\beta_1)^{1/2}}\frac{I}{p_2} \qquad (A.2)$$

$$q_3^{IP} = (\overline{q}_3+h)+\mu(\beta_1/\varepsilon)-\rho\, r \qquad (A.3)$$

$$P_1 = p_1q_1 - w(q_1/b_1)^2 - \overline{C}_1 \qquad (A.4)$$

$$P_2 = p_2q_2 - w(q_2/b_2)^2 - \overline{C}_2 \qquad (A.5)$$

$$P_3 = p_3q_3^{IP} - w(q_3^{IP}/b_3)^2 \qquad (A.6)$$

$$\frac{w}{p_1} = \frac{b_1^2}{2q_1} \qquad (A.7)$$

$$\frac{w}{p_2} = \frac{b_2^2}{2q_2} \qquad (A.8)$$

$$\frac{w}{p_3} = \frac{b_3^2}{2q_3} \qquad (A.9)$$

$$T_L = \left(\frac{q_1}{b_1}\right)^2 + \left(\frac{q_2}{b_2}\right)^2 \qquad (A.10)$$

$$T_L = (T-l)-\left(\frac{a\varepsilon}{2wA}\right)^{2/3}I^{4/3} \qquad (A.11)$$

where $A = \left\{(p_1\beta_1)^{1/2}+(p_2\beta_2)^{1/2}\right\}^2$

$$q_3^{IP} = b_3(1-a)^{1/2}(T_L^*)^{1/2} \qquad (A.12)$$

$$I = (P_1+\overline{C}_1)+(P_2+\overline{C}_2)+wT_L \qquad (A.13)$$

$$M(\beta_1/\varepsilon, cc, re, H)V = p_1(q_1+\frac{p_2}{p_1}q_2) \qquad (A.14)$$

(A.1) and (A.2) are a household's demand functions for Good 1 and Good 2, (A.3) is the equilibrium condition (supply equals demand) for the pure investment good based on the loanable funds theory (the definition of firms' demand for pure investment goods), (A.4), (A.5), and (A.6) are the profit functions for each of a firm's production divisions, (A.7), (A.8), and (A.9) are the firm's supply functions for Good 1, Good 2, and Good 3 based on profit maximization, (A.10) is the equilibrium condition (supply equals demand) for the labor market, (A.11) is a household's labor supply function based on Equation 4.12, (A.12) gives the level of production of the pure investment good based on households' investment of their savings, (A.13) defines total household income including profit distributions and compensation for fixed costs, and (A.14) is the equilibrium condition (supply equals demand) for the money market based on the quantity theory of money (the so-called "transactions version" of the quantity equation).

The above framework consists of 14 equations in 13 unknown variables, which means that we are dealing with an overdetermined system of equations. However, provided that (A.10)—the equilibrium condition for the labor market—holds, q_2 is automatically determined once q_1 and T_L are determined, such that (A.2)—the demand function for Good 2—can be omitted in accordance with Walras' Law. This leaves us with 13 equations in 13 unknown variables, which can be solved as follows:

(Solutions to equations)

$$q_1^* = \left\{ \frac{(\beta_1/b_1)^{2/3}}{(\beta_1/b_1)^{2/3}+(\beta_2/b_2)^{2/3}+(a\varepsilon)^{2/3}} \right\}^{1/2} b_1(T-I)^{1/2}$$

$$q_2^* = \left\{ \frac{(\beta_2/b_2)^{2/3}}{(\beta_1/b_1)^{2/3}+(\beta_2/b_2)^{2/3}+(a\varepsilon)^{2/3}} \right\}^{1/2} b_2(T-I)^{1/2}$$

$$q_3^{IP*} = b_3(1-a)^{1/2} \left\{ \frac{(\beta_1/b_1)^{2/3}+(\beta_2/b_2)^{2/3}}{(\beta_1/b_1)^{2/3}+(\beta_2/b_2)^{2/3}+(a\varepsilon)^{2/3}} \right\}^{1/2} (T-I)^{1/2}$$

$$\left(\frac{w}{P_1}\right)^* = \left\{ \frac{(\beta_1/b_1)^{2/3}+(\beta_2/b_2)^{2/3}+(a\varepsilon)^{2/3}}{(\beta_1/b_1)^{2/3}} \right\}^{1/2} \frac{b_1}{2(T-I)^{1/2}}$$

$$\left(\frac{P_2}{P_1}\right)^* = \left(\frac{\beta_2}{\beta_1}\right)^{1/3} \left(\frac{b_1}{b_2}\right)^{4/3}$$

$$\left(\frac{P_3}{P_1}\right)^* = (1-a)^{1/2} \frac{b_1}{b_3} \left\{ \frac{(\beta_1/b_1)^{2/3}+(\beta_2/b_2)^{2/3}}{(\beta_1/b_1)^{2/3}} \right\}^{1/2}$$

$$P_1^* = \frac{1}{2}\left\{\frac{(\beta_1/b_1)^{2/3}}{(\beta_1/b_1)^{2/3}+(\beta_2/b_2)^{2/3}}\right\}M(\beta_1/\varepsilon,cc,re,H)V - \overline{C_1}$$

$$P_2^* = \frac{1}{2}\left\{\frac{(\beta_2/b_2)^{2/3}}{(\beta_1/b_1)^{2/3}+(\beta_2/b_2)^{2/3}}\right\}M(\beta_1/\varepsilon,cc,re,H)V - \overline{C_2}$$

$$P_3^* = \frac{1}{2}(1-a)M(\beta_1/\varepsilon,cc,re,H)V$$

$$I^* = M(\beta_1/\varepsilon,cc,re,H)V$$

$$T_L^* = \frac{(\beta_1/b_1)^{2/3}+(\beta_2/b_2)^{2/3}}{(\beta_1/b_1)^{2/3}+(\beta_2/b_2)^{2/3}+(a\varepsilon)^{2/3}}(T-l)$$

$$r^* = \frac{1}{\rho}\left\{(\overline{q_3}+h)+\mu\beta_1/\varepsilon - b_3(1-a)^{1/2}(T_L^*)^{1/2}\right\}$$

$$p_1^* = \frac{M(\beta_1/\varepsilon,cc,re,H)V}{b_1\left\{1+(\beta_2/\beta_1)^{2/3}(b_1/b_2)^{2/3}\right\}^{1/2}(T_L^*)^{1/2}}$$

Note that the solution for T_L^* is our "basic equation of labor" (Equation 4.28).

The above microeconomic framework can easily be generalized to the case of more than two consumption goods (which are also renewal investment goods).

As we discussed in Chapter 4, most variables in the above framework—including the level of employment, output quantities for each good, relative prices, the interest rate, and the price level (price of the reference good)—depend on the relative utility attrition rate β_1/ε and ratios of utility attrition rates such as β_2/β_1. This means that the levels of the utility attrition rates (parameters for households that correspond to the level of human desire for each consumption good) play a vital role —together with the productivity parameters in firms' production functions—in determining the levels of variables.

1.2. A Summary from the Perspective of Macroeconomic Theory

In this book we have presented two macroeconomic frameworks: a basic framework based on (traditional) classical macroeconomic theory (developed in Chapter 4), and a revised framework based on the concept of "controllable loan balances" (developed in Chapter 6). We summarize each of these frameworks below based on the assumption of a perfect employment equilibrium (i.e. no downward rigidity of the money wage).

Note that horizontal bars are used to denote parameters of the models.

Model 1: basic framework

$$F'(T_L) = w/p \qquad\qquad (B.1)$$

$$T_L = L(w/p, \overline{\beta/\varepsilon}, \overline{a}) \qquad\qquad (B.2)$$

$$Y = F(T_L) \qquad\qquad (B.3)$$

$$S_W(\overline{\beta/\varepsilon}, \overline{a}) = I_P(\overline{\beta/\varepsilon}, r) + \overline{G} \qquad\qquad (B.4)$$

$$M(\overline{\beta/\varepsilon}, \overline{H})\overline{V} = pY \qquad\qquad (B.5)$$

β/ε denotes the relative utility attrition rate for the reference good, a denotes the average propensity to consume, S_W denotes household savings, I_P denotes pure investment, G denotes government spending, Y denotes gross domestic product, w/p denotes the real wage, T_L denotes labor time, r denotes the natural interest rate, M denotes the money supply (in stock terms), H denotes high-powered money, V denotes the velocity of money, and p denotes the price level (the price of the reference good).

(B.1) is the firm's labor demand function based on the first postulate of classical macroeconomic theory (the wage is equal to the marginal product of labor), (B.2) is the household's labor supply function, (B.3) is the macroeconomic production function, (B.4) is the equilibrium condition (supply equals demand) for the pure investment good based on the loanable funds theory, and (B.5) is the equilibrium condition (supply equals demand) for the money market based on the quantity theory of money (the so-called "transactions version" of the quantity equation).

There are five endogenous variables: w/p, T_L, Y, r, and p. w/p and T_L are first determined by solving (B.1) and (B.2). Y is then determined by substituting the solution for T_L into (B.3), and p is then determined by substituting the solution for Y into (B.5). r is determined independently by (B.4).

This process of determining the endogenous variables is based on classical macroeconomic theory, and satisfies the so-called "classical dichotomy" in that real variables are all determined in real markets irrespective of what happens in the money market. However, the solution for each of the endogenous variables depends on β/ε (the relative utility attrition rate for the reference good), which means that all of the endogenous variables are affected by human demand psychology.

Model 2: revised framework based on the concept of "controllable loan balances"

$$F'(T_L) = w/p \qquad\qquad (C.1)$$

$$T_L = L(w/p, \beta/\varepsilon, \overline{a}) \qquad\qquad (C.2)$$

$$Y = F(T_L) \tag{C.3}$$

$$S_W(\beta / \varepsilon, \bar{a}) + \overline{\Delta M} = I_P(\beta / \varepsilon, r_m) + \overline{G} \tag{C.4}$$

$$\beta / \varepsilon = \overline{\beta_r / \varepsilon} + R(\overline{G}) + R(r_m) \tag{C.5}$$

$$M(\beta / \varepsilon, \overline{H})\overline{V} = pY \tag{C.6}$$

β / ε denotes the relative utility attrition rate for the reference good, β_r / ε denotes real utility attrition, R denotes monetary utility attrition, a denotes the average propensity to consume, S_W denotes household savings, I_P denotes pure investment, G denotes government spending, Y denotes gross domestic product, w/p denotes the real wage, T_L denotes labor time, r_m denotes the market interest rate, M denotes the money supply (in stock terms), H denotes high-powered money, V denotes the velocity of money, p denotes the price level (the price of the reference good), and ΔM denotes credit creation by the banking system in line with monetary policy action.

(C.1) is the firm's labor demand function based on the first postulate of classical macroeconomic theory (the wage is equal to the marginal product of labor), (C.2) is the household's labor supply function, (C.3) is the macroeconomic production function, (C.4) is the equilibrium condition (supply equals demand) for the pure investment good based on the loanable funds theory, and (C.6) is the equilibrium condition (supply equals demand) for the money market based on the quantity theory of money (the so-called "transactions version" of the quantity equation). (C.5) defines the relative utility attrition rate as the sum of real utility attrition and monetary utility attrition. Real utility attrition is a given parameter, while monetary utility attrition is defined as a function of the market interest rate and government spending.

There are six endogenous variables: β / ε, w/p, T_L, Y, r_m, and p. β / ε and r_m are first determined by solving (C.4) and (C.5) as a pair of simultaneous equations. (C.1) and (C.2) can then be used to express w/p and T_L as functions of β / ε, and substituting the function for T_L into (C.3) allows Y to be expressed as a function of β / ε. The solution for β / ε can then be used to determine w/p, T_L, and Y. Finally, p is determined by substituting the solutions for β / ε and Y into (C.6).

The classical dichotomy does not apply to this framework, as fiscal and monetary policy measures cause interactions between the money market and the labor and goods markets (as well as the loan market). It should also be noted that all endogenous variables are influenced by β_r / ε (real utility attrition), G (government spending), and ΔM (credit creation by the banking system in line with monetary policy action).

1.3. Characteristics of Our Theoretical Framework

The aim of this book has been to construct a theoretical framework for the study of economics that better reflects the importance of various psychological factors and the causal connections between them. In other words, we have sought to improve the ability of economic theory to analyze various economic phenomena by explicitly modeling those elements of human desire that represent the true essence of any economy. In this section we summarize some key characteristics of the theoretical framework that we have developed with these objectives in mind.

(1) Our overall framework is founded on a "basic human accounting" framework that illustrates the interdependence of various "accounts"—utility, goods, work time, and money—with a view to illustrating the importance of various psychological factors and the causal connections between them. This underlying framework has enabled us to construct models of both non-monetary and monetary economies in which psychological factors are endogenized.

(2) Our analysis is based on an economic model that emphasizes time factors, and assumes that utility attrition (the process by which utility from goods diminishes over time)—rather than the initial endowment of production factors, pure investment, or government spending—is the fundamental driver of demand (economic activity).

(3) As in traditional economic theory, we have considered subjective equilibria based on the assumption that households are utility maximizers and firms are profit maximizers. We have constructed a framework in which the utility attrition rate simultaneously determines both the level of employment (output) and the allocation of resources based on the process by which households maximize their expected total utility (defined as the sum of expected utility from goods and utility from leisure). Our "basic equation of labor" describes the relationship between the utility attrition rate and the level of employment, and we have shown that this equation is identical for non-monetary and monetary economies alike in our model.

(4) In order to demonstrate the direct relationship between human psychology (desire) and economic fluctuations, we have demonstrated the existence of an endogenous economic cycle driven by the existence of goods with non-linear increasing-gradient utility attrition functions and the inverse relationship between the level of household employment (or output levels) and the utility attrition rate (the fundamental driver of demand).

(5) We have introduced the concept of "controllable loan balances" as a means of extending (traditional) classical macroeconomic theory to allow for interactions between real markets and the money market as a result of monetary utility attrition.

(6) We have presented a formal theoretical justification for "discriminatory spending policy", in which subsidies are paid to those households that are most likely to make additional purchases of consumption goods.

(7) Finally, we have constructed separate frameworks for real utility attrition and monetary utility attrition, and have emphasized the importance of policies that recognize the role of real utility attrition in long-term economic growth.

2. A Brief Discussion of Underemployment Equilibrium Analysis

2.1. The Labor Market and Downward Rigidity of Money Wages

In this section we briefly discuss an important topic that we have been unable to consider in greater detail in this book: underemployment equilibrium analysis for the case where the money wage exhibits downward rigidity.[1]

Let us now suppose that a firm's labor demand function (expressed in terms of the real wage) is as shown by curve D in Figure 8.1(b), and that a household's labor supply function is as shown by curve S in Figure 8.1 (b). The equilibrium real wage $(w/p_1)^*$ and the equilibrium work time (employment level) T_L^* are determined by the intersection of curves D and S (point e).

The equilibrium shown in Figure 8.1(b) is the "full employment" equilibrium of classical economic theory (which implicitly assumes that all households are already working), whereby all households with the will and capacity to work at the prevailing wage level are gainfully employed. The total supply of labor (from all households) is actually greater than the equilibrium employment level T_L^*, but there is "voluntary unemployment" corresponding to work that would be done for no other reason than to maintain survival if the prevailing wage were to fall below the equilibrium wage $(w/p_1)^*$. According to Keynes (1936), there may also be "frictional unemployment" resulting from insufficient information or movements of labor between industries, but if such unemployment is ignored, then a labor market with a Walrasian price adjustment mechanism is always (automatically) in a state of full employment.

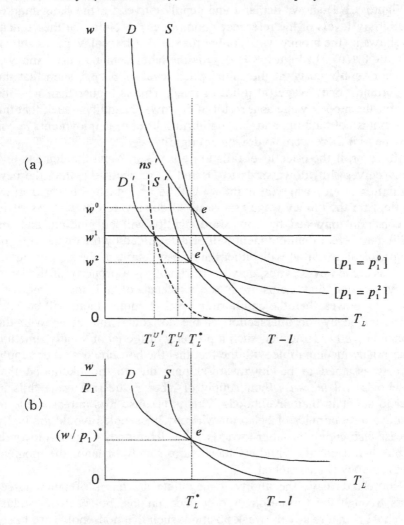

Figure 8.1 Demand and supply curves for the labor market for arbitrary levels of the reference good price (p_1) and the impact of the existence of downward rigidity of money wages to the equilibrium level of employment

However, if the money wage exhibits downward rigidity (as discussed in Keynes), then depending on the price level p_1 (the price of the reference good), then the (given) floor for the money wage w_1 may be higher than the equilibrium money wage w^*, such that the Walrasian price adjustment mechanism breaks down, and the equilibrium employment level is less than the level at the "full employment" equilibrium (T_L^*).

Figure 8.1(a) shows demand and supply curves for the labor market for arbitrary levels of the reference good price (p_1). Note that the vertical axis shows w (the money wage) rather than w/p_1 (the real wage, as shown in Figure 8.1(b)). In Figure 8.1(a), D is the labor demand curve and S is the labor supply curve at the initial price level of $p_1=p_1^0$, such that the equilibrium money wage (at point e) is w^0. This is higher than w^1—the floor for the money wage as a result of downward rigidity—such that the constraint is not binding, and the equilibrium level of employment (T_L^*) is the same as if there were no downward rigidity.

However, if the price level falls to $p_1=p_1^2$ ($< p_1^0$) and the demand and supply curves shift downwards to D' and S' respectively, then the new equilibrium money wage (at point e') will be w^2, which is lower than w^1 (the floor for the money wage as a result of downward rigidity). As such, the constraint imposed by downward rigidity will be binding, and the equilibrium level of employment will be determined by the intersection of the horizontal line at w^1 with either the demand curve or the supply curve.

If, as argued by Keynes, downward rigidity is a property of the labor supply function that stems from the existence of a labor union with bargaining power, then the equilibrium level of employment will be $T_L^{U'}$, as determined by the intersection of the horizontal line at w^1 with the demand curve D'. However, such a property of the labor supply function is essentially incompatible with the fact that the household's labor supply curve is assumed to be downward-sloping due to the likelihood that households will *increase* their supply of labor if the real wage falls in order to maintain their livelihoods. This is because it is unreasonable to assume a discontinuity of behavior whereby households would gradually increase their supply of labor towards T_L^U as the money wage fell towards w^1, but then suddenly withdraw their entire supply of labor the moment that the money wage reached w^1.

Households have the ability to negotiate the terms of labor agreements through the formation of organized unions, but each individual household is in a relatively weak position, such that households are likely to act defensively—despite the existence of unions—by increasing their supply of labor in the face of declines in the real wage with a view to maintaining a certain level of income.

The ability of households to withdraw their supply of labor by calling a strike in response to a reduction of the money wage is sometimes cited as the reason why the labor supply is elastic at a given level of the money wage and why the money wage exhibits downward rigidity. In practice, however, a strike does damage to a firm's reputation and financial performance, and thereby threatens the livelihood of all striking union members (as well as any non-union employees). As such, it is perhaps best to regard (the threat of) strikes as a negotiating tactic that is used by organized labor unions rather than as an inherent characteristic of households' labor supply behavior.

It is therefore necessary to view downward rigidity of the money wage as a property of the firm's labor demand function if we are to consider downward rigidity in a consistent fashion within our theoretical framework. This could be explained in terms of a labor agreement that requires firms to keep the demand price for labor (the money wage) at or above a certain level. In other words, we consider a labor agreement negotiated between firms and households that requires firms to maintain a certain level of the money wage. This represents a constraint on firms: even if the marginal productivity of labor decreases as a result of an increase in the employment level (the number of hours worked by households), firms are not able to lower the money wage in order to fully maximize their profits. Such a state of affairs is at odds with Keynes' argument, in that demand for labor is a function of the money wage—and not a decreasing function of the real wage—once the level of employment (work hours) exceeds a certain level, which means that demand for labor can be elastic for a given level of the money wage. Under this framework, the equilibrium level of employment will be T_L^U, as determined by the intersection of the horizontal line at w^1 with the supply curve S' in Figure 8.1(a). This equilibrium employment level (T_L^U) lies along the labor supply curve that is determined by the subjective equilibria of households, such that unemployment may be viewed as a "voluntary" consequence of a fall in the price of the reference good that has boosted the household's real wage (for the given level of w^1).

2.2. Corporate Profit Trends and Labor Adjustments (in Terms of Household Numbers)

We next consider the subjective equilibria of (profit-maximizing) firms, and show that the classical assumption (that all households are already working) only holds true if there is no downward rigidity of the money wage in the labor market, and that where downward rigidity does exist, the best option for a firm is for it to abandon its right to accept offers of labor supply from all households and limit itself to offers from a certain group or range of households.

Figure 8.2 shows—for a given price level—the relationship between the level of labor demand as determined by the money wage and corporate profits under the profit-maximizing behavior of firms.

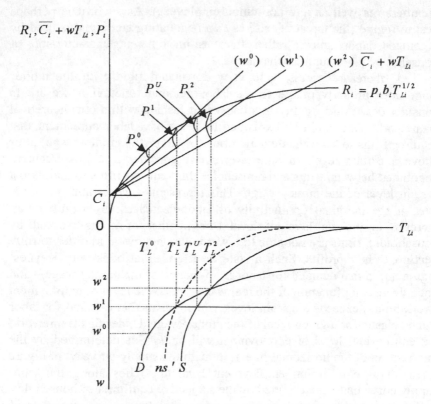

Figure 8.2 Relationship between the level of labor demand as determined by the money wage and corporate profits under the profit-maximizing behavior of firms

w^0, w^1, and w^2 are various levels of the money wage (where $w^0 > w^1 > w^2$), T_L^0, T_L^1, and T_L^2 are the corresponding levels of labor demand based on the profit-maximizing behavior of firms, and P^0, P^1, and P^2 are the corresponding levels of corporate profits.

Where there is no downward rigidity, $P^2(w^2) > P^1(w^1) > P^0(w^0)$, such that corporate profits increase as the equilibrium money wage—as determined by the labor supply curve—falls. In order for firms to make the equilibrium money wage as low as possible, they must ensure that the labor supply curve lies as far to the right as possible, that is, they must impose no restriction on employment and accept offers of labor supply from all households. In other words, the classical assumption (that all households are already working) holds true if there is no downward rigidity of the money wage in the labor market.

However, if firms are required to maintain a labor demand price (money wage) of w^1 as a result of a labor agreement, then they will no longer be able to earn P^2, the level of profits that corresponds to a money wage of w^2 and an equilibrium employment level of T_L^2. Instead, they will earn P^U, which corresponds to the equilibrium employment level T_L^U as determined by the intersection of the horizontal line at w^1 with the supply curve S. Because $P^U(w^1) < P^2(w^2)$, the firm will face a reduced profit or possibly a loss due to the lack of a wage adjustment mechanism, and may therefore face a financial crisis.

One possible way for the firm to overcome this crisis might be for it to enter into a work-sharing agreement or some other agreement designed to reduce total work hours, such that households would voluntarily reduce their supply of labor so that the labor supply curve S would shift downwards to the point where it intersected the labor demand curve D at w^1, the fixed money wage. However, it is likely that such an arrangement would be difficult to implement in a timely fashion given the concerns that firms would have regarding reduced labor productivity and the concerns that households would have regarding a reduction of their total wage income.

As such, the best option for a firm is for it to abandon its right to accept offers of labor supply from all households and limit itself to offers from a certain group or range of households, thereby bringing about an adjustment to the number of households that it employs.[2]

Suppose that there are N households in the economy (society) in question, and that n of these households are working at the prevailing level of the real wage. The labor supply curve S can be derived by multiplying the supply curve for the representative household s' by N along the horizontal axis. Where the number of households is adjusted so as to realize the firm's subjective equilibrium, just n households (corresponding to the curve ns' in Figure 8.2 and 8.1) are employed at the prevailing level of the money wage w^1, such that the remaining $N-n$ are involuntarily unemployed, that is, they are not employed despite being willing and able to work at the prevailing real wage. The equilibrium level of employment in this case will be $T_L^{U'}$ as shown in Figure 8.1(a), such that the amount of involuntary unemployment will be equal to $T_L^U - T_L^{U'}$. However, the firm is once again able to realize its subjective equilibrium as a result of this adjustment to the number of households that it employs, thereby increasing its profits from $P^U(w^1)$ back to $P^1(w^1)$.

It should be clear from the above that while a decline in the price level in Figure 8.1(a) for a fixed money wage (w^1) initially results in voluntary unemployment equal to $T_L^* - T_L^U$, the resulting equilibrium (the subjective equilibrium of households) is unstable because it differs from the subjective equilibrium of firms. As such, it cannot be sustained, and involuntary unemployment equal to $T_L^U - T_L^{U'}$ will eventually arise as a result of adjustments to the number of households employed by firms.[3]

We have therefore shown that the classical assumption (that all households are already working) does not hold true if there is downward rigidity of the money wage in the labor market, in which case the best option is for firms to adjust (reduce) the number of households that they employ.

3. Directions for Future Research

We conclude this chapter with a brief discussion of important areas that we have been unable to cover in this book.

(1) Analysis of related goods (complements and substitutes) or superior/
inferior goods

In this book we have used the relationship between the budget constraint and goods preference curves to examine how demand for each good reacts to changes in household income or the prices of goods. In doing this, we have assumed that utility attrition rates are independent, such that the utility attrition rate for a given good is not affected by demand for other goods or the level of household income. However, in cases where two goods are complements (substitutes), an increase in demand for one good would cause the utility attrition rate for the other good to increase (decrease). Furthermore, the utility attrition rate for a superior good (inferior good) could be expected to increase (decrease) as a result of an increase in household income. Extension of our framework to allow for analysis of resource allocations in the case of related goods (complements and substitutes) or superior/inferior goods is a matter for future research.

(2) Construction of a model including tax rates, and analysis based on
that model

Future research could also extend our framework to allow for inclusion (specification) of taxation rates for income tax, corporation tax, and other taxes, thereby enabling analysis of how changes to the taxation regime may affect the economy via changes to labor's (and capital's) share of income and changes to household's average propensity to consume.

(3) Construction of an open economy model, and analysis based on that model

The analysis in this book is based on a closed economy that has no trade (import/export) or capital transactions with other countries (economies). Extension of our framework to allow for analysis of an open economy is a matter for future research. This would require "basic human accounting" frameworks for each country (monetary economy) to be linked together, after which it would be necessary to derive a "basic equation of labor" for the open economy model. This equation could then be used to examine the relationship between utility attrition (desire) and the equilibrium employment levels in the home economy and its trading partners, and examine the implications of changes in utility attrition rates for a nation's trade surplus, exchange rates, and economic growth.

(4) Short-term analysis taking the impact of financial assets into account

As we discussed in Section 3.1 of Chapter 1, the analysis in this book is based on long-term flows, and does not consider the impact of stock levels, such that the supply of labor and demand for goods are viewed as two sides of the same coin. However, the existence of financial assets that have been accumulated over time can enable households to (temporarily) increase their demand for goods without increasing their supply of labor. It remains to be seen how the conclusions of this book might be affected if the impact of financial assets were to be recognized and the supply of labor and demand for goods were to be coupled incompletely.

NOTES

1. Formalization based on a mathematical model and other details have been left for future research.
2. Specific methods of adjusting the number of households could include tighter age restrictions, stricter requirements with regard to qualifications, requiring offers to be made in certain ways, or shortening the offer period.
3. The same idea is applicable even if analysis is based on the upward-sloping labor supply curve of classical macroeconomic theory.

References

A. Foreign Language References

Ackley, G. (1961), *Macroeconomic Theory*, New York: Macmillan (*Makurokeizaigaku no Riron (I)(II)(III)*; supervised and translated by Tsuru, S., Tokyo: Iwanami Shoten, 1964-69).

Blaug, M. (1978), *Economic Theory in Retrospect*, 3rd edition, Cambridge University Press, chapters 6-8 (*Shinban/ Keizai Riron no Rekishi (II)—Kotten Gakuha no Kakumei*, translated by Sugihara, S. and S. Miyazaki, Tokyo: Toyo Keizai Shinpo-sha, 1984).

Defoe, D. (1719), *The Life and Strange Surprising Adventures of Robinson Crusoe (Robinson HyouRyuuki*, translated by Yoshida, K., Tokyo: Shinchosha, 1951).

Ferguson, C. E. and S. C. Maurice (1974), *Economic Analysis*, revised edition, Homewood, Ill.: Irwin (*Keizai Bunseki Nyuumon*, first and last volume, translated by Kimura, K., Tokyo: Nihon Hyouronsha, 1975-76).

Gordon, R. J. (1974), *Milton Friedman's Monetary Framework: A Debate with His Critics*, Chicago: University of Chicago Press (*Friedman no Kahei Riron— Sono Tenkai to Ronsou*, translated by Kato, H., Tokyo: McGraw-Hill Kougakusha, 1978).

Hall, T. E. and J. D. Ferguson (1998), *The Great Depression: An International Disaster of Perverse Economic Policies*, University of Michigan (*Daikyoukou—Keizai Seisaku no Ayamari ga Hikiokoshita Sekaitekina Saiyaku*, translated by Miyagawa, S., Tokyo: Taga-shuppan, 2000).

Henderson, J. M. and R. E. Quandt (1971), *Microeconomic Theory: A Mathematical Approach*, 2nd edition, New York: McGraw-Hill (*Gendai Keizaigaku—Kakaku Bunseki no Riron*; revised edition, translated by Komiya, R. and H. Kanemitsu, Tokyo: Soubunsha, 1973).

Hicks, J. R. (1946), *Value and Capital: An Inquiry into Some Fundamental Principles of Economic Theory*, 2nd edition, Oxford: Clarendon Press (*Kachi to Shihon—Keizai Riron no Jyattukan no Kihongenri ni Kansuru Kenkyu*, first and last volume, translated by Yasui, T. and H. Kumagai, Tokyo: Iwanami Shoten, 1995).

170   *References*

Hicks, J. R. (1950), *A Contribution to the Theory of the Trade Cycle*, Oxford: Clarendon Press (*Keikijyunkanron*, translated by Furuya, H., Tokyo: Iwanami Shoten, 1951).

Keynes, J. M. (1936), *The General Theory of Employment, Interest and Money, The Collected Writings of John Maynard Keynes*, Vol.VII, 1973 (*Koyou Rishi oyobi Kahei no Ittupan Riron*, popularized edition, translated by Shionoya, Y., Tokyo: Toyo Keizai Shinpo-sha, 1995).

Klein, L. R. (1947), *The Keynesian Revolution*, New York: Macmillan (*Keynes Kakumei*, translated by Shinohara, M. and K. Miyazawa, Tokyo: Yuhikaku, 1965).

Knight, F. H. (1921), *Risk, Uncertainty and Profit*, Iowa, seventh impression, 1948 (*Kiken Fukakujitusei oyobi Rijyun*, translated by Okuzumi, E., Tokyo: Bungado-shoten, 1959).

Robbins, L. C. (1932), *An Essay on the Nature and Significance of Economic Science*, Macmillan (*Keizaigaku no Honshitu to Igi*, translated by Tsuji, R., Tokyo: Toyo Keizai Shinpo-sha, 1957).

Samuelson, P. A. (1947), *Foundations of Economic Analysis*, Harvard University Press (*Keizai Bunseki no Kiso*, translated by Sato, R., Tokyo: Keiso-shobo, 1967).

Say, J. B. (1821), *Catéchisme d' économie politique, ou instruction familière qui montre de quelle façon les richesses sont produites, distribuées et consommées dans la société (Letters to Mr. Malthus on several subjects of political economy and on the cause of the stagnation of commerce, to which is added A catechism of political economy, or, Familiar conversations on the manner in which wealth is produced, distributed, and consumed in society)*, translated by John Richter, New York: A. M. Kelley, 1967, reprint (originally published: London: Neely & Jones, 1821), pp. 19-20.

Say, J. B. (1836), *A Treatise on Political Economy*, with a new introduction by Munir Quddus and Salim Rashid, New Brunswick: Transaction Publishers, 2001; New York: A. M. Kelley, 1971, reprint (originally published by Grigg & Elliot, 1836), pp. 387-391.

Schumpeter, J. A. (1912), *Theorie der wirtschaftlichen Entwicklung*, Leipzig (*Keizai Hattuten no Riron*, first and last volume, translated by Shionoya, Y., Nakayama, I., and S. Tohata, Tokyo: Iwanami Shoten, 1977).

Smith, A. (1776), *An Inquiry into the Nature and Causes of the Wealth of Nations*, London, edition by E. Cannan 1904, Parts 1-3 (*Syokokumin no Tomi*, Vols 1-5, translated by Ouchi, H. and S. Matsukawa, Tokyo: Iwanami Shoten, 1959-60).

B. Japanese References

Ara, K. (1985), *Lecture on Macro Economics (Macro Keizaigaku Kougi)*, Tokyo: Soubunsha.

Asano, E. (1976), *A Guide for Learning "The General Theory" by J. M. Keynes (Keynes Ittupanriron Nyumon)*, Tokyo: Yuhikaku.

Datai, T. (1989), *A Model-based Analysis of the History of Economic Theory (Keizaigakusetushi no Model Bunseki)*, Fukuoka: Kyushyu University Press.

The Economic Planning Agency (ed.) (1997), *Annual Report on the Japanese Economy 1997 (Keizai Hakusyo, Heisei 9 nendoban)*, The Ministry of Finance Printing Bureau.

Fujita, K. (1995), *The World of Economic Equilibrium (Keizai Kinkou no Sekai—Mono to Kane no Jyunkan no Kagaku)*, Kyoto: Sagano Shoin.

Hirasawa, N. (1995), *Lecture on the Basic Theory of Macroeconomics (Macro Keizaigaku Kisoriron Kougi)*, Tokyo: Yuhikaku.

Imai, K., Uzawa, H., Komiya, R., Negishi, T., and Y. Murakami (1971), *Price Theory (I) (Kakaku Riron (I))*, Tokyo: Iwanami Shoten.

Inoue, Y. (1993), *Principles for the Study of the Market Economy (Shijyou Keizaigaku no Genryu)*, Tokyo: Chuo Kouronsha.

Itou, M. (1962), *Keynes—The birth of a "new economics" (Keynes— "Atarashii Keizaigku" no Tanjyou)*, Tokyo: Iwanami Shoten.

Itou, M. and M. Nei (1993), *Schumpeter—A Proudly Independent Economist (Schumpeter—Kokou no Keizaigakusha)*, Tokyo: Iwanami Shoten.

Kagawa, A., Tsubonuma, H., and T. Kataoka (1999), *First Steps in Macro Economics (First Step Macro Keizaigaku)*, Tokyo: Yuhikaku.

Kanaya, S. (1992), *Monetary Economics (Kahei Keizaigaku)*, Tokyo: Shinseisha.

Kimura, K. (1973), *Macro Economic Theory (Kyositeki Keizairiron)* revised edition, Tokyo: Nihon Hyouronsha.

Kobayashi, R., Hirose, K., and F. Sato (1974), *An Introduction to Mathematical Analysis (Kaisekijyosetsu)*, Tokyo: Kyouritsu-shuppan.

Komiya, R. and A. Amano (1972), *International Economics (Kokusai Keizaigaku)*, Tokyo: Iwanami Shoten.

Maki, A. (1983), *Consumer Preference and Measurement of Demand (Syouhi Senkou to Jyuyou Sokutei)*, Tokyo: Yuhikaku.

Miyazaki, Y. and M. Itou (1961), *Commentary on the General Theory of J. M. Keynes (Commentary, Keynes Ittupan Riron)*, Tokyo: Nihon Hyouron sya.

Nakayama, I. (1937), *The Study of Mathematical Economics (Suuri Keizaigaku Kenkyu)*, Tokyo: Nihon Hyouron sya.

Nishikawa, S. (1974), *Economics (Keizaigaku)*, Tokyo: Toyo Keizai Shinpo-sha.

Nishikawa, S. (1988), *Economics (Keizaigaku)*, 3rd edition, Tokyo: Toyo Keizai Shinpo-sha.

Oobuchi, T. (author and editor) (1977), *Modern Economics (Gendai Keizaigaku)*, Tokyo: Yachiyo-shuppan.

Oshima, M. (1947), *Lecture on Philosophy (Tetsugaku no Hanashi)*, Tokyo: Houbunkan.

Shimamura, H. (1997), *Macroeconomics—Theory and Policy (Macro Keizaigaku—Seisaku to Riron)*, Tokyo: Seibundou.

Shionoya, T. (1963), *Commentary on "The General Theory" by J. M. Keynes, Based on the Original Text (Genten Keynes "Ittupanriron" Kaisetsu)*, Tokyo: Syunjyuu-sha.

Shirakawa, K. (1988), *The Economics of Added Value (Fukakachi no Keizaigaku)*, Tokyo: Tsukuba-shobo.

The Society of Modern Economics (ed.) (1966), *Marx and Keynes—The World's 15 Foremost Economics (Marx and Keynes Sekai Jyuugodai Keizaigaku)*, Tokyo: Fuji-shoten.

The Society of Modern Economics, Sato, T. and K.Yajima (eds.) (1970), *The 10 Foremost Schools of Economics and the Continuation of the World's 15 Foremost Economics (Jyuudai Keizai Gakuha to Zoku Sekai Jyuugodai Keizaigaku)*, Tokyo: Fuji-shoten.

Sugimoto, E. (1950), *An Explication of Modern Economic—its Genealogy and Current Evaluation (Kindai Keizaigaku no Kaimei—SonoKeifu to Gendaiteki Hyouka)*, Tokyo: Riron-sha.

Takekuma, S. (1998), *The Basic Theory of Macroeconomics (Macro Keizaigaku no Kisoriron)*, Tokyo: Shinsei-sha.

Uzawa, H. (1977), *A Reexamination of Modern Economics (Kindai Keizaigaku no Saikentou)*, Tokyo: Iwanami Shoten.

Watanabe, Y. (1998), *The Endogenous Money Supply Theory—Post Keynesian Approach (Naiseiteki Kaheikyoukyuu Riron—Post Keynes ha Apurouchi)*, Tokyo: Taga-shuppan.

Index